The Illustrated ENCYCLOPEDIA of the IRISH SEASHORE

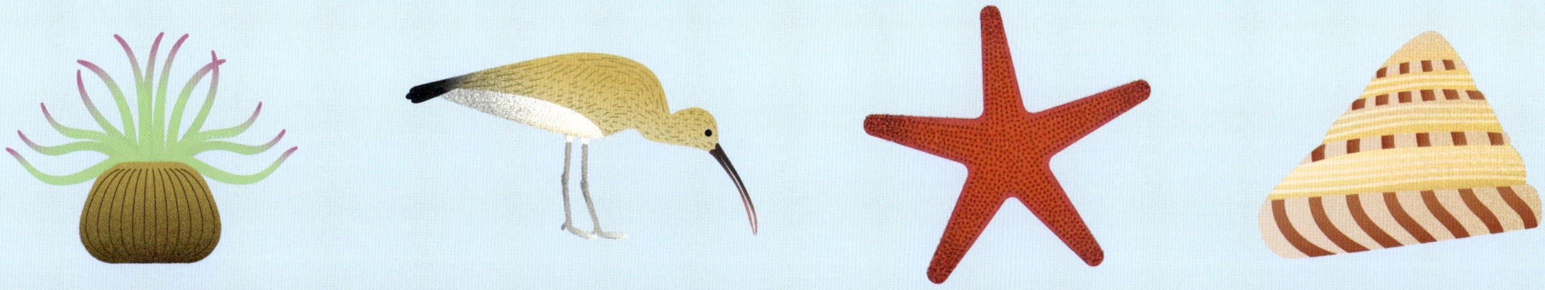

The Illustrated ENCYCLOPEDIA of the IRISH SEASHORE

Written by

LUCY TAYLOR

Illustrated by

LINDA FÄHRLIN

Gill Books
Hume Avenue
Park West
Dublin 12
www.gillbooks.ie

Gill Books is an imprint of M.H. Gill and Co.

978 1804 58325 8

Designed by Graham Thew © Gill Books
Edited by Jessica Spencer
Proofread by Anna Kealy
Printed and bound by L.E.G.O. SpA, Italy
This book is typeset in 12pt on 15pt, New Spirit

The paper used in this book comes from the wood pulp of sustainably managed forests.

To the best of our knowledge, this book complies in full with the requirements of the General Product Safety Regulation (GPSR). For further information and help with any safety queries, please contact us at productsafety@gill.ie.

A CIP catalogue record for this book is available from the British Library.

5 4 3 2 1

For permission to reproduce photographs, the author and publisher gratefully acknowledge the following:

© Adobe Stock: Ernie Cooper, 21; cascoly2, 49; © Alamy: Nature Picture Library, 17; Laurie Campbell, 25; Nigel Sawyer, 27; Major Archive, 53 © Shutterstock: emka74, 15; RugliG, 51.

The author and publisher have made every effort to trace all copyright holders, but if any have been inadvertently overlooked we would be pleased to make the necessary arrangements at the first opportunity.

FSC
www.fsc.org
MIX
Paper | Supporting responsible forestry
FSC® C023419

Contents

What is the seashore?

The seashore is where land and sea overlap. It is uncovered at the lowest tides and covered by the highest tides.

For many of us, the seashore is a place to explore, play, swim and relax. It is also home to hundreds of types of plants and animals that live buried in the sand, floating in the water, in tidal rock pools or clinging to rocks.

It is difficult to measure the length of Ireland's seashore, but we estimate that it is about 5,800km long, which is longer than the distance between Dublin and New York.

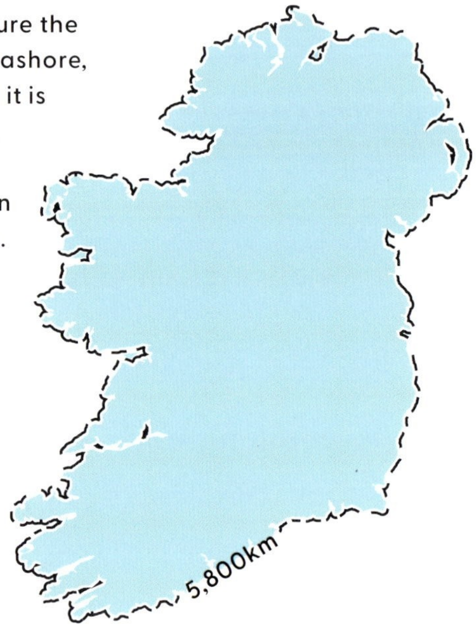

Coastal land is influenced by strong, salty winds and seawater. Coastal seas contain soil and fresh water from the land. Land temperatures change more quickly than water temperatures, so on the seashore, the sea heats up and cools down more than in the open ocean.

The Irish seashore

Life in Ireland has always been closely linked with the sea and the seashore. Seashores have provided food for communities who eat seaweed, shellfish and fish since people arrived on the island thousands of years ago. Before there were roads, people used boats and travelled along rivers, lakes and the coast. Anyone leaving or arriving in Ireland used the sea until the twentieth century. Our coast is what connects us to the rest of the world.

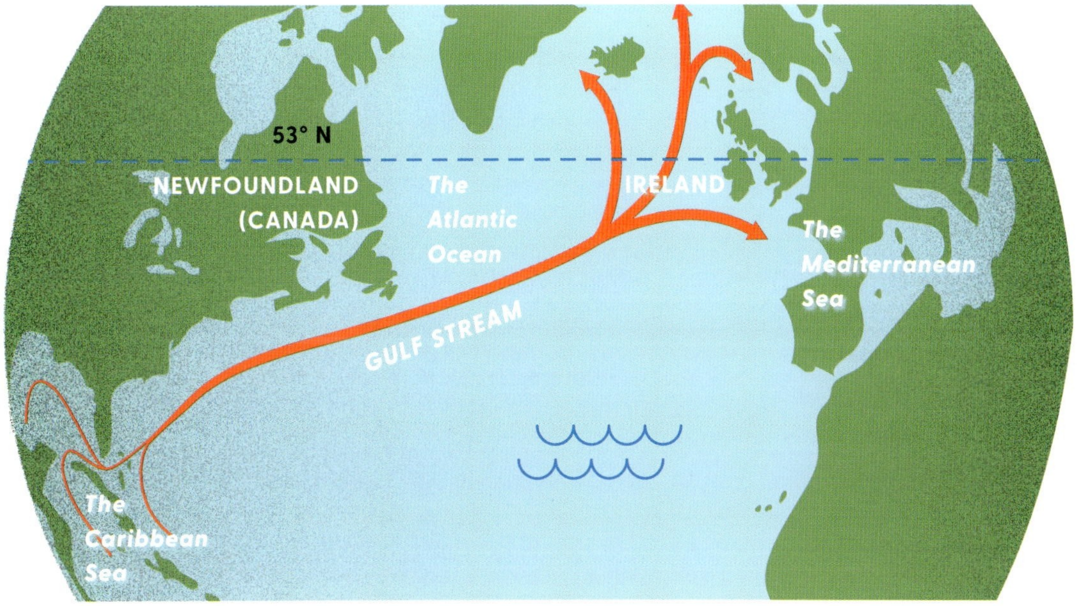

Atlantic waters

Ireland is located in the north-east Atlantic at a latitude of roughly 53°N. At a similar latitude on the western edge of the Atlantic, around Newfoundland in Canada, the seawater can dip to below freezing. This never happens in Ireland because of an ocean current that carries warm water north-east from the Caribbean Sea. This keeps our Atlantic waters slightly warmer, especially in the south-west of the island. This unique position means that Ireland is home to some seashore species that are also found in the Arctic, and some that are also at home in the warmer Mediterranean.

As the climate changes, sea temperatures are increasing. Initially, this means we will have warmer water, but in the long term it could also mean that the ocean currents change.

Tides

Tides are like extremely slow waves that come from the open ocean towards our coastlines and make the sea level rise and fall. The tide comes in and out every six hours.

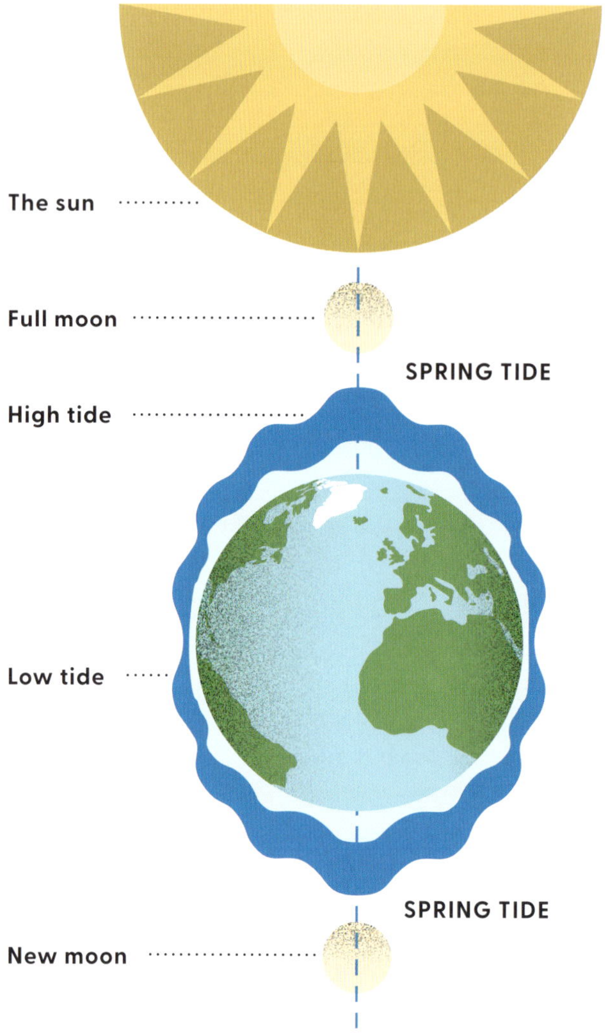

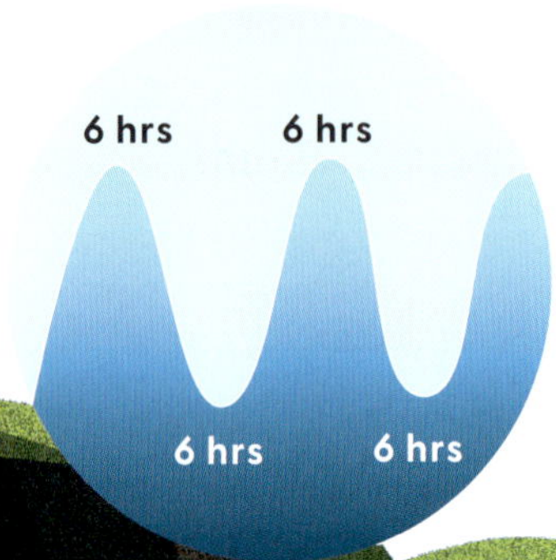

What causes tides?

We know that the earth has gravity that enables us to keep our feet on the ground whether we are in the Arctic or Australia. Like the earth, the moon and the sun also have a gravitational pull. Their gravity also pulls our oceans and causes tides. The earth circles the sun at a consistent speed, and the moon circles the earth consistently as well, so we can predict the height of the tide depending on where we are in relation to the sun and the moon.

Spring tides and neap tides

The highest tides and lowest tides occur when the sun, the moon and the earth are aligned. This happens twice a month: when there is a full moon and when there is a new moon. These are called spring tides. The gravitational pull of the moon and the sun combines and causes the earth's water to bulge outwards. Neap tides occur when the difference between high and low tide is at its smallest. These happen twice a month when there is a quarter moon.

Tides in different places

Tides are also affected by lots of other factors, including the shape of the earth (which isn't a perfect sphere), the shape of the ocean floor, and ocean currents.

For example, the difference between high and low tide can be bigger in bays or estuaries, where the water is pushed into a narrow channel. The difference between high and low tide in Dublin Bay looks very different to the Cliffs of Moher because the shore in Dublin Bay is almost completely flat and the Cliffs of Moher are vertical.

The tide also changes as we go around the island, so some places never experience tides as big as in other places.

Before you visit your favourite beach, you can check tide time tables online or in a book to see when the tide will be in or out. A low tide gives you more space on the beach and for exploring the rock pools and seashore!

The difference between high and low tide in the south-east is about 1.75 metres. On the west coast it is more than twice that.

Zones on the seashore

Because the tide comes in and out twice a day in Ireland, plants and animals on the seashore will experience completely different conditions depending on where they live.

Zonation

We can divide seashores into zones based on how often the tide covers each area and how often that area is exposed to the air. Some species can survive being out of the water for hours, while others will not survive if they are underwater for long periods. Throughout this book we will learn about where on the shore you are likely to find certain plants and animals.

Splash zone

The highest part of the shore is the splash zone. The tide never completely covers this area. Sand dunes, clifftops and the grassy area at the top of some sandy beaches are often in the splash zone. We still think of the splash zone as the seashore because it gets salty spray from the wind and it might be splashed or covered by the biggest waves or during a storm. Anything that lives here has to be able to survive in a dry, salty, windy environment.

Marram grass has waxy leaves and can 'spit out' salt to survive on a sandy beach.

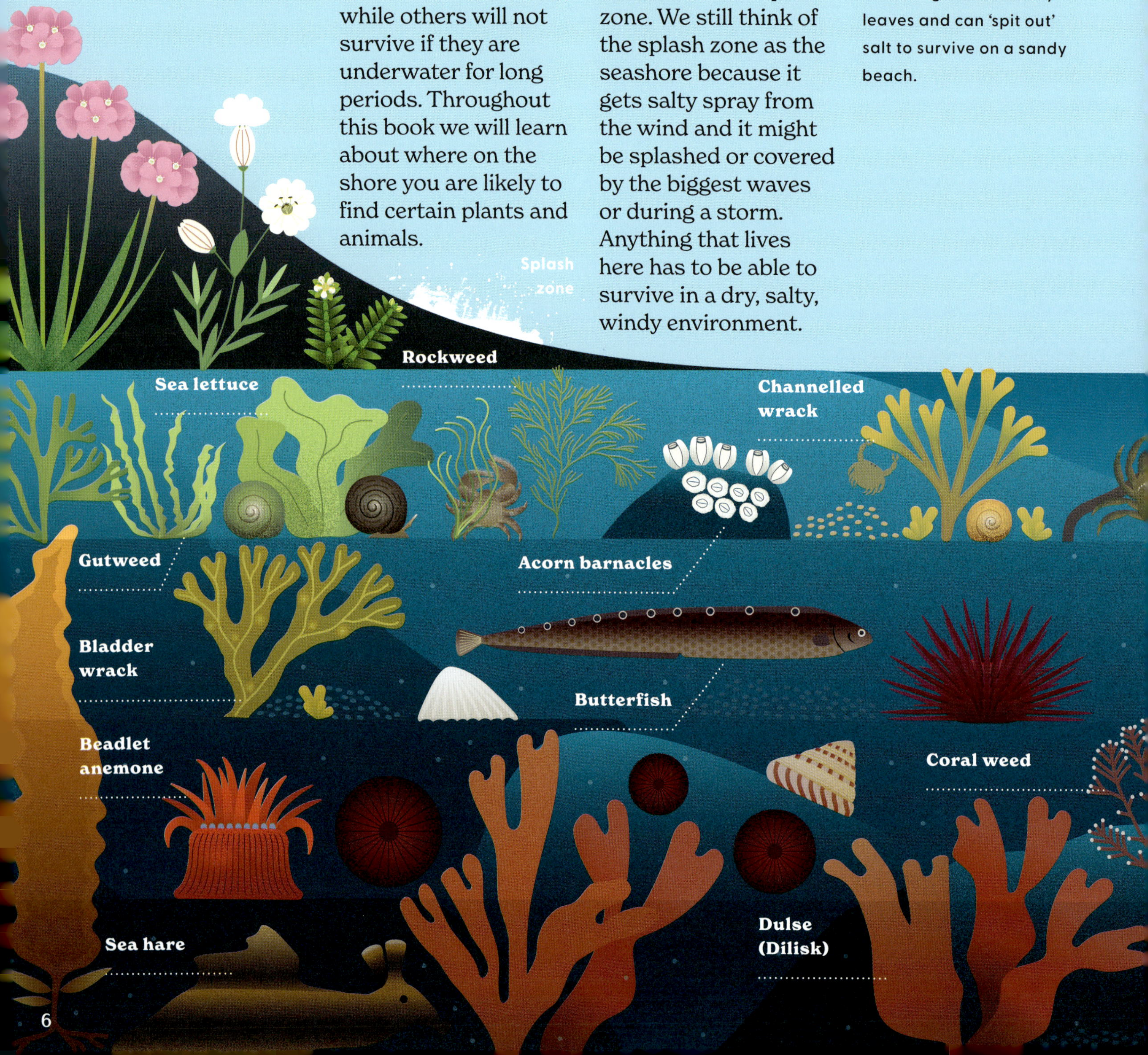

Upper shore
The upper shore is covered when the tide is at its highest, which only happens every few weeks. Sometimes you might notice a line along rocks and cliffs near the sea that shows where this zone is. You might also notice a line on the beach where the highest tides have dropped seaweed and shells.

Middle shore
The middle shore is covered and uncovered twice a day by the tide. On rocky shores, the rock pools in this zone are often full of life. On sandy beaches, this is the area where the sand is just a little bit wet almost all of the time.

Lower shore
The lower shore is almost always underwater except at the lowest tides. Anything that lives here is suited to life in the water, not in the air.

Subtidal zone
The subtidal zone is always underwater, but at very low tides you might be able to paddle here or explore with a net and a bucket. You might find fish and other animals that can't survive out of the water.

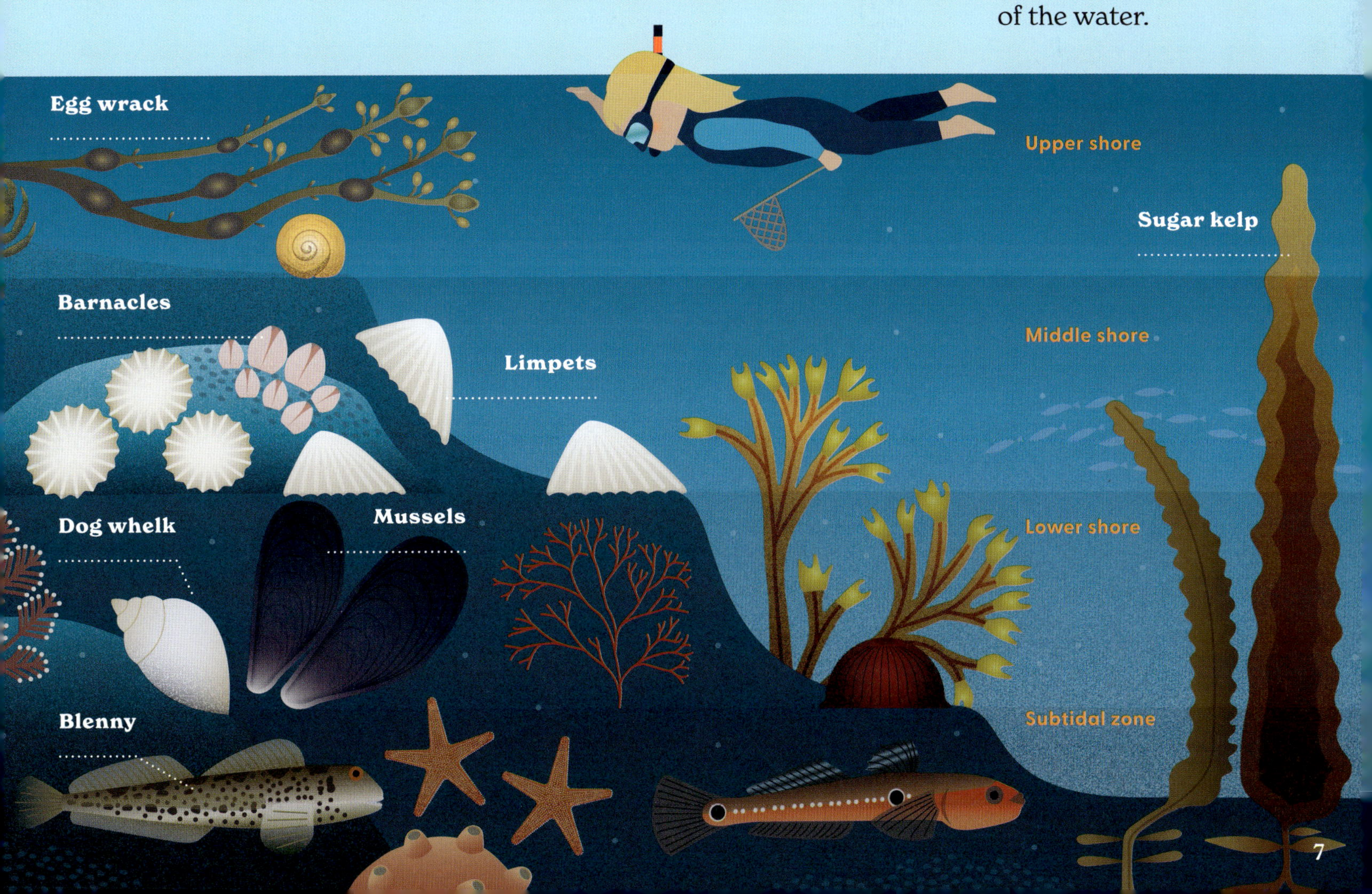

Surviving on the seashore

Life in the sea is very different to life on land. To live on the seashore, many animals need to survive in both environments.

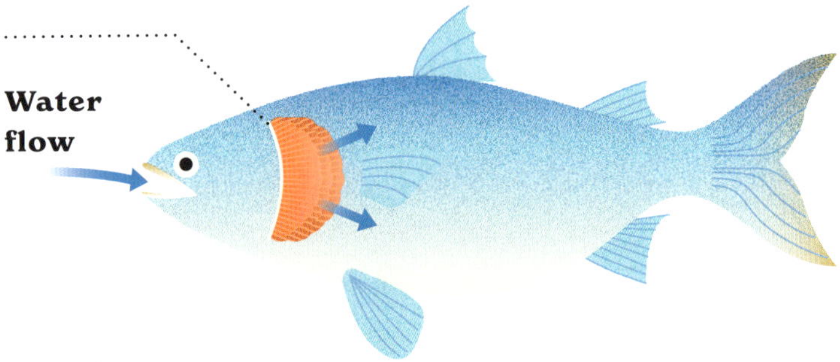

Lungs and gills

Our lungs are perfectly adapted to extract oxygen from air. Most marine animals have gills, which are adapted to extract oxygen from water. On the seashore, many animals, such as the shore crab and some fish, are left out of water when the tide goes out. They are able to stay alive as long as they stay damp and cool.

Temperature changes

Water heats up and cools down more slowly than air. This means that marine animals are used to quite consistent temperatures. However, if you live in a rock pool, the temperature can change dramatically. At low tide in the summer, the water can get quite warm. Warm water holds less oxygen, so being in a warm rock pool is probably like being in a stuffy room with no windows. This can be stressful for marine species.

If you find an animal sheltering under a rock or seaweed, don't move it out into the sunshine, as it will quickly become very stressed.

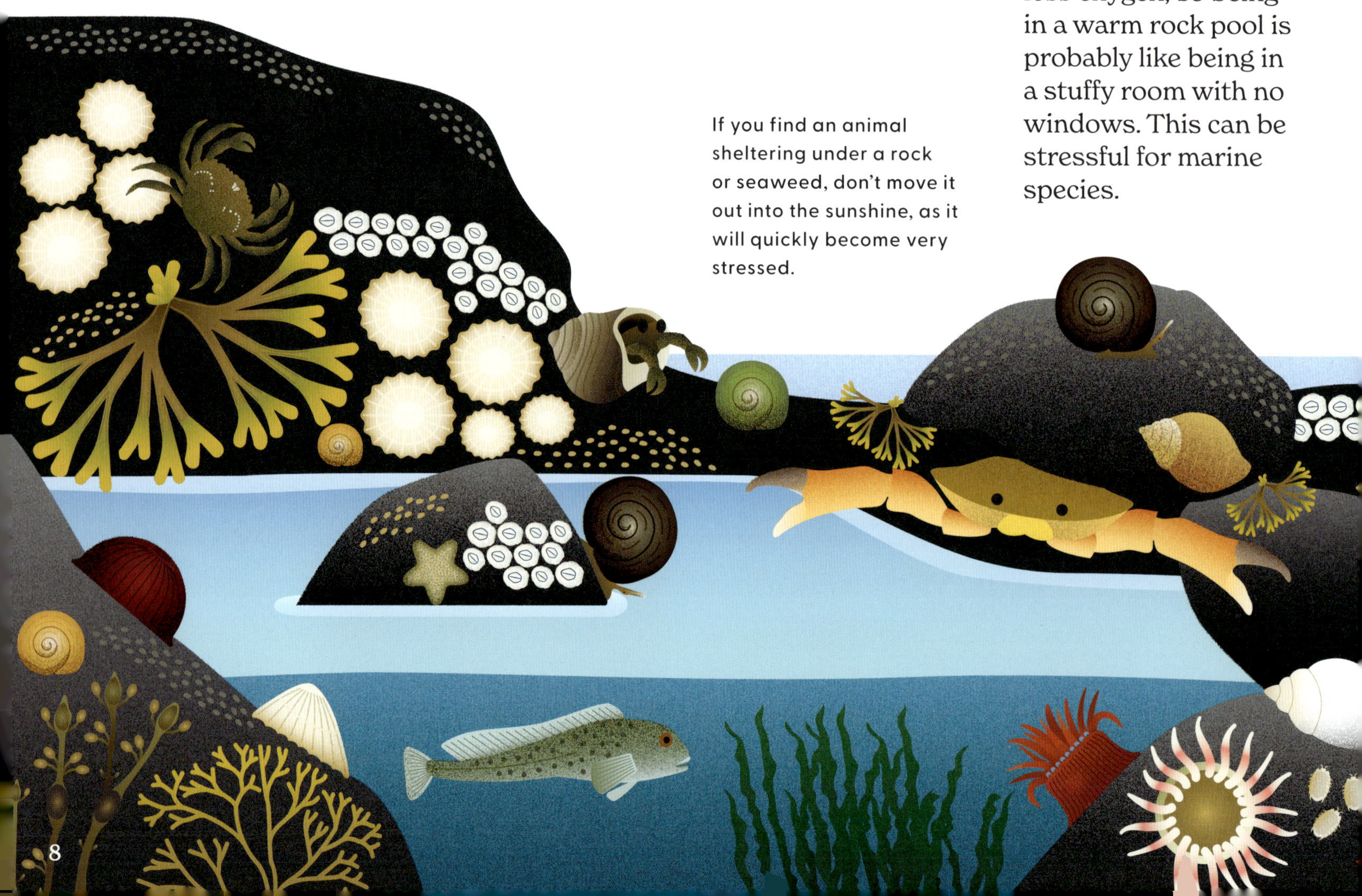

Feeding

For creatures living in the sea, water provides oxygen, but it also carries microscopic plants, animals and nutrients. Many marine creatures just stick out their arms or open their mouths and wait for the right food to float by. Seaweeds can absorb what they need from the water around them.

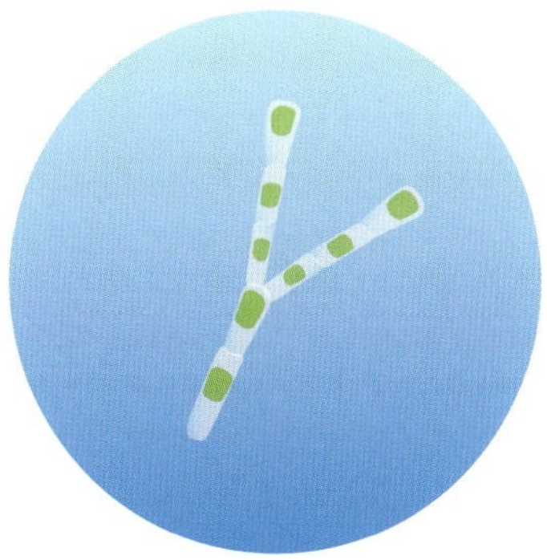

Microscopic plant

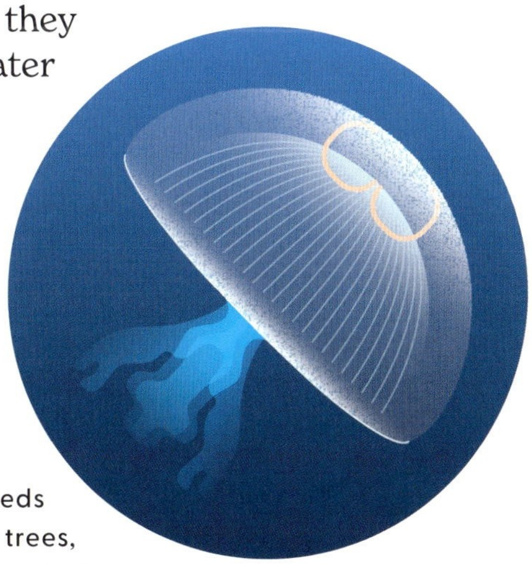

In the water, many marine animals have no need for heavy skeletons, and seaweeds don't have trunks like trees, because they are supported by the water around them.

Salty waves

Seawater is very salty. Out in the ocean, the level of salt is consistent, but on the seashore, it can change a lot. Rainfall and rivers add fresh water and reduce the level of salt. On a warm day water might evaporate from rock pools, leaving them much saltier. Only those plants and animals that can adapt to these changeable conditions are able to survive on the seashore.

Another big challenge on the seashore is surviving crashing waves. Finding shelter, moving to deeper water or having a shell strong enough to avoid being crushed are all important strategies for seashore survival.

The reasons why so many plants and animals live along the seashore is that the water here is often richer in nutrients than further out at sea and there are hard surfaces to cling to. It isn't all bad!

The limpet has a shell to protect itself and a suction cup to help stay in place.

Seashore habitats

A habitat is a place where a plant or animal likes to live. Seashores in Ireland vary from spectacular cliffs that stand tall against the power of the Atlantic Ocean to sheltered sandy beaches that change with every tide.

Rocky shores
Rocky shores are some of the most diverse seashore habitats. In sheltered places, the entire rocky shore is covered in seaweed, barnacles and limpets. Rock pools can be full of fish, shrimps and marine snails. In exposed places the rock is bare.

Sand dunes
Sand dunes occur just above the high tide, but they are closely linked to the seashore. They are created by plants such as marram grass and are home to many birds and other animals. They are very delicate, but they also protect our coastlines from storms.

Sandy beaches
Sandy beaches are difficult places to live because the sand moves so easily. Animals that make sandy beaches their home usually live buried under the surface. The high tide line is often a great place to look for things that have been washed in by the sea, such as shells and mermaid's purses.

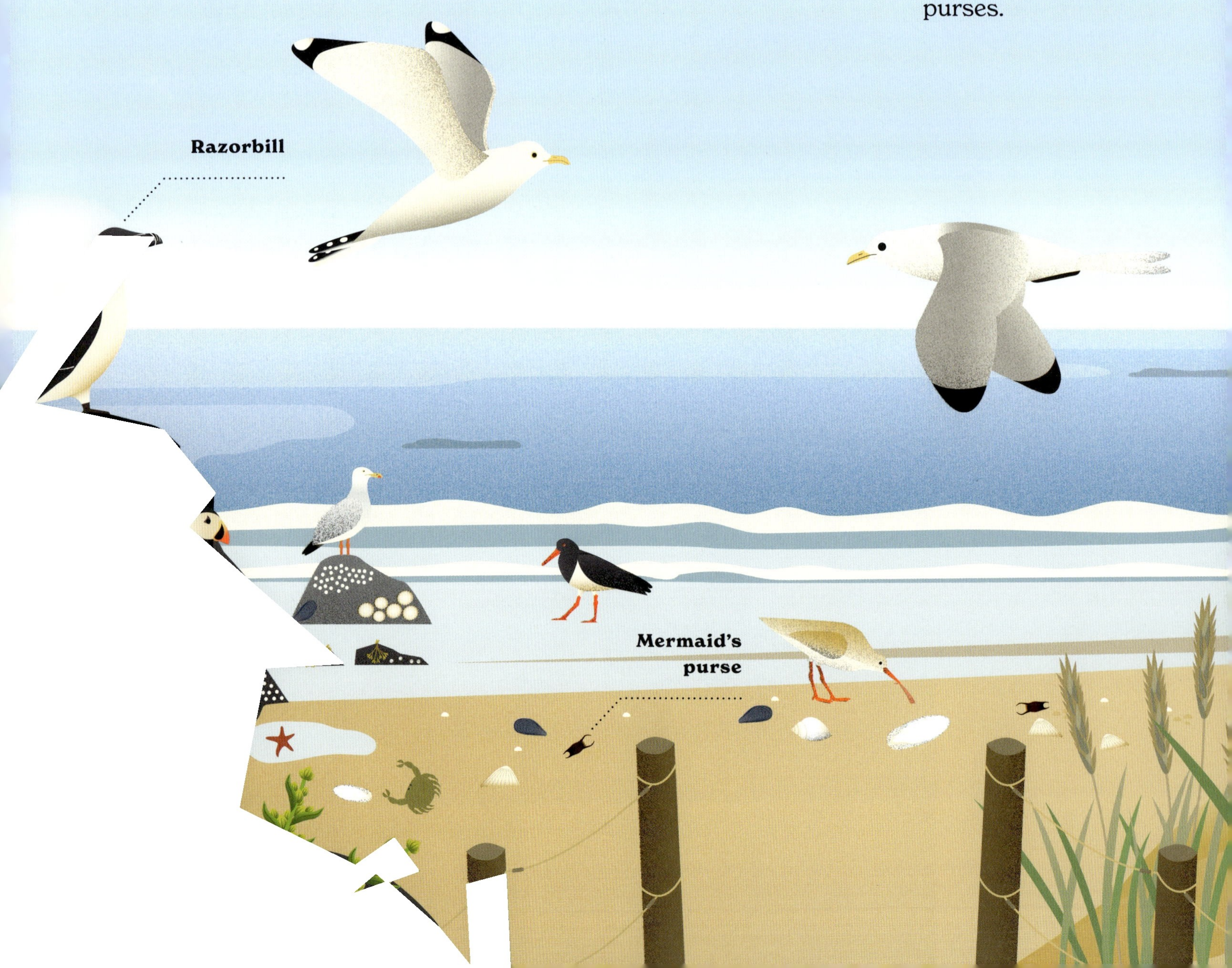

Estuaries and wetlands
An estuary is where a river meets the sea. As they meet, the river flow slows down and the tiny bits of soil and sediment it carries sink to the ground. This creates an abundance of nutrients for animals that can survive in the mix of fresh and salty water. The animals that live buried in the sand are a delicious feast for many birds and larger animals like dolphins, fish and otters.

Wetlands and marshes are always flooded. They are interesting places to look for birds hiding among the rushes and other plants while they feed on the many tasty things that live in the muddy ground.

Pebble beaches
It is extremely difficult to find anywhere safe to live between the moving stones on a pebble beach. However, in very sheltered areas they do get covered in seaweed and some shellfish can settle in among the stones. In other places they are called storm beaches because stones get thrown onto the beach during stormy weather – but the stones don't stay still long enough for anything to live on them. Next time you visit a pebble beach, try to decide if you think it's sheltered or not.

Seashore plants

Irish shores are home to a beautiful selection of plants that have adapted to the salty, dry, windy, splashy and generally quite extreme environment just above the high tide mark.

Tough leaves

Even though we think of seashores as wet places, being covered in salt actually makes it very difficult for plants to hold onto water. As a result, many plants that can survive on the shore have developed leaves that can tolerate salt water or the drying effect of strong coastal winds. Sandy or stony shores and dunes don't hold water at all, and marshes or wetlands are always soggy, so many plants have adapted their roots to one or other of these extremes.

Why are seashore plants important?

Plants are also very important on the seashore, as their roots help to hold sand together and protect against erosion and damage from storms. Their leaves also catch and hold sand, helping to build dunes. The plants attract butterflies and moths and provide shelter for nesting birds and other animals. Many of these plants can also be eaten by people and are used in traditional herbal remedies.

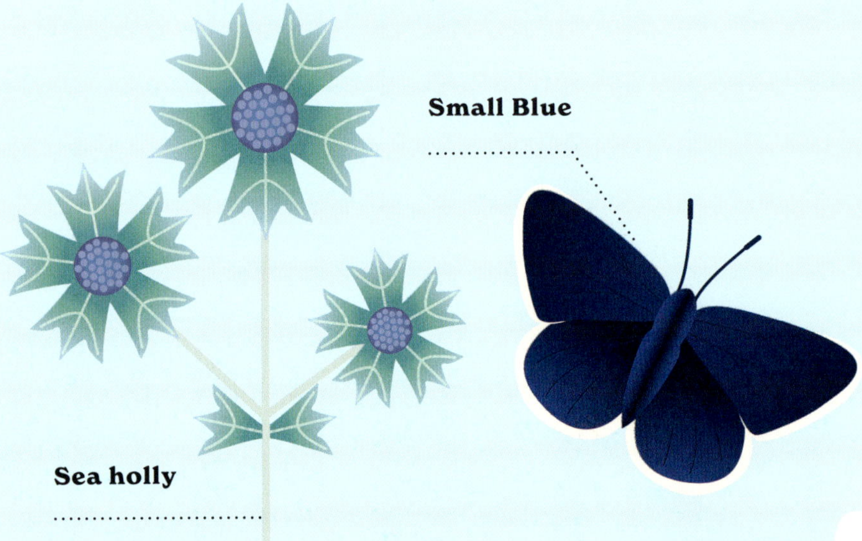

Rocky shore plants

Sea pinks (also known as thrift), campion and rock samphire are examples of plants that are tough enough to grow in tiny crevices on rocky shores and cliffs.

Sea pinks and campion both create cushiony clumps of tough roots and leaves along rocky coasts and cliffs. Samphire grows out of rocky crevices and has thick, fleshy leaves that have a lemony taste.

Sand, dune and pebble shore plants

Sea beet grows among pebbles and stones and has shiny, waxy leaves that can be eaten like spinach. Orache also has pointed leaves, but usually isn't shiny. Sea sandwort is tiny, but extremely tough and can creep very quickly through sand on the upper shore. Sea mayweed has flowers like giant daisies and very delicate leaves. Sea holly is distinctive – it has spiky bluish leaves and bright blue flowers.

The leaves of marram grass are pointed, waxy and curled. Inside the curled surface, tiny hairs help to hold onto moisture. The roots grow deep down into dunes and form dense, matted networks that hold the plant in place and hold the dune together. Sea bindweed often curls in among other plants on dunes and has large pink and white flowers, the colour of strawberry-and-vanilla ice cream!

Sea beet

Orache

Sea mayweed

Marram grass

Sea sandwort

Coastal mammals

Mammals are our closest relatives – like us, they give birth to live young and feed them on milk. Ireland's native mammals include: hares that graze on coastal fields and dunes; whales and dolphins that live entirely in the ocean; seals and otters that move between the land and water; and foxes and stoats that sometimes visit shores to feed.

Whales and dolphins

It is always exciting to see a whale or a dolphin. The ocean around Ireland is home to quite a few different species, including the enormous blue whale. However, from the seashore you are more likely to see small animals such as the harbour porpoise. You might spot the small triangular fins on their backs as they 'porpoise' through the water. Common dolphins also often travel and feed quite close to shore and can put on spectacular displays as they leap out of the water and move in large pods. Bottlenose dolphins are large – up to four metres long.

Foxes and stoats might also visit seashores to scavenge or hunt. Stoats are very small – smaller than a cat – and very quick and nimble compared to otters.

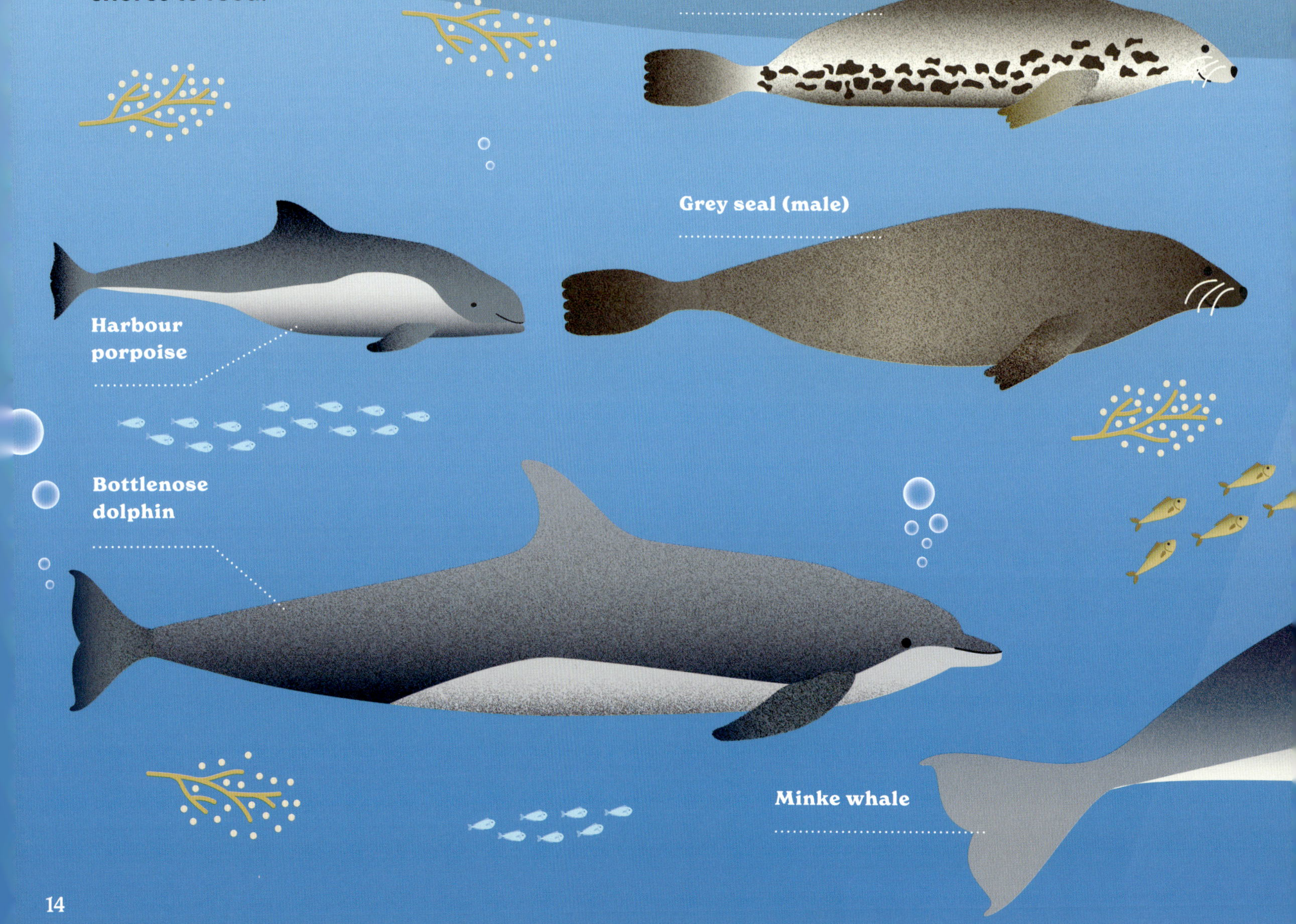

Grey seal pup

Seals

Ireland has two species of seal – harbour seals and grey seals. Harbour seals are smaller and have faces that look a bit like a big dog's face. Grey seals are much bigger and their faces are a different shape – more like the shape of a horse's face. You might spot seals resting on rocks or popping their heads out of the water to peek at you. Harbour seals give birth in the spring and summer and the pups are able to swim just a few hours after they're born. Grey seals give birth in the autumn. Grey seal pups are white and fluffy and stay on shore for the first two or three weeks. Their mums will leave to go fishing and then return to feed their pups. They are vulnerable when they are alone, so we should be careful not to disturb them.

Otters

Otters live near water all across Ireland, but in coastal places they often hunt in the sea for fish, crabs and other shellfish. They then return to their dens on land, so you might spot their footprints on beaches. Otters are also very vocal and the cubs scream and squeal loudly as they fight and play.

Blue whale

Harbour seal

There are resident bottlenose dolphins in the Shannon estuary.

Seashore birds

Ireland is famous for its populations of seabirds and many of them are strongly connected to the seashore.

Crows

Several of Ireland's eight crow species visit seashores. One, the red-billed chough, is truly coastal. Choughs have bright red legs and beaks. They are rare globally, but on parts of Ireland's coast, these glossy, loud birds live in large groups. Choughs nest on cliffs and in old buildings and forage on seashores and in rough coastal fields and dunes.

Waders

Seashores, estuaries and wetlands are full of food for those birds that know how to find it. Waders move through water with long legs and probe wet ground with their long beaks to find worms and shellfish. Oystercatchers are perhaps the most distinctive, with their smart black-and-white feathers and their cartoonishly long red beak and legs. They are sometimes joined by small sandpipers or ringed plovers that run along the edge of the waves. Larger waders such as curlews can reach deep into wet sand to find food. Our shores are a perfect stopover for birds that need to rest and feed as they migrate in spring and autumn.

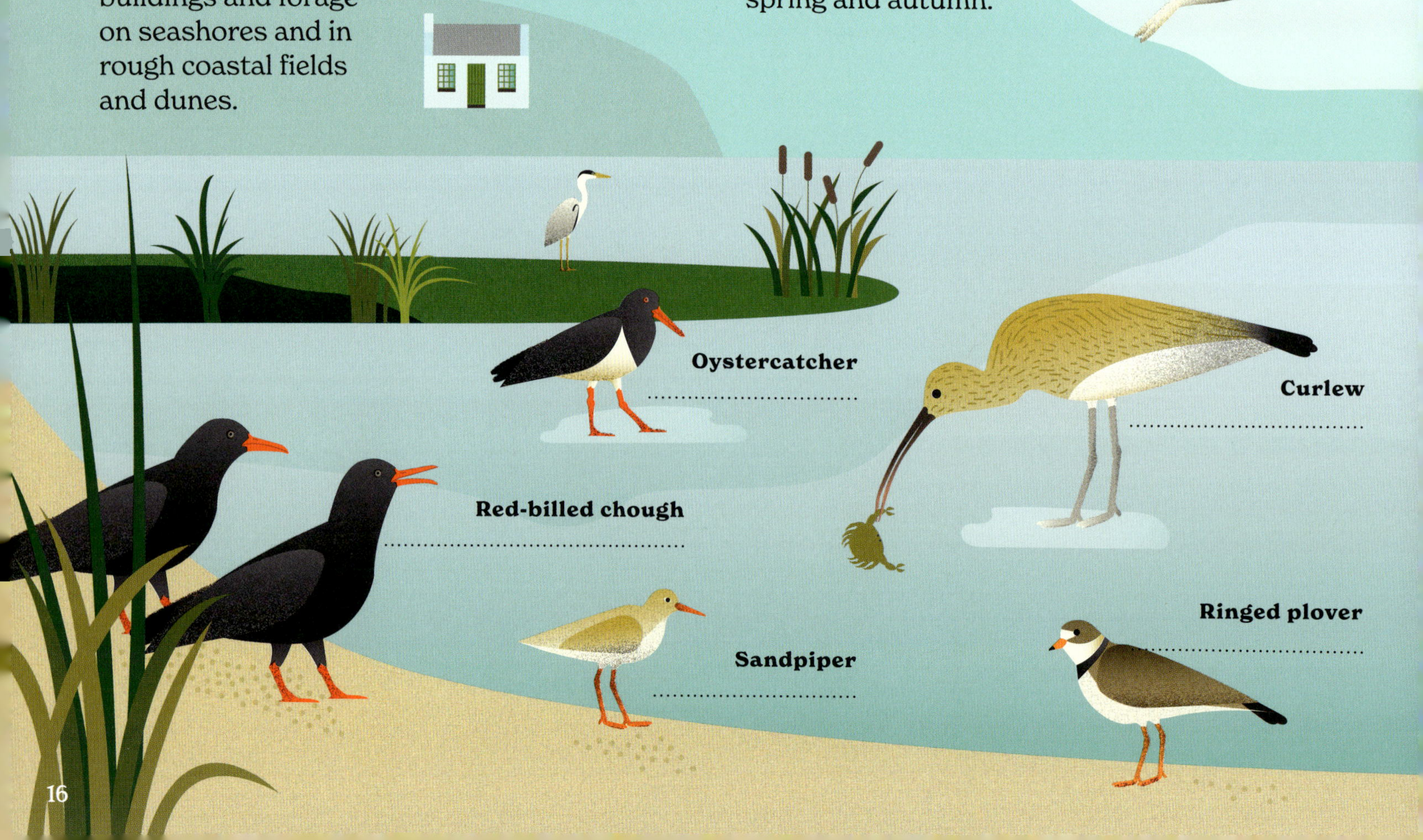

Gulls

Ireland has about twelve different species of gull and they can be tricky to tell apart. They are all a combination of white and grey or black. They are generally loud and full of personality! As well as eating fish and shellfish, many gulls are scavengers. You might see gulls chasing other birds and annoying them so much that the other birds drop their food. They sometimes try this same trick on people who are eating chips or ice cream!

Cormorants and shags

These elegant black birds nest on cliffs and in high trees along the coast. Unusually for waterbirds, their feathers aren't waterproof, so they perch on rocks and hold their wings open to dry them – a bit like Dracula holding open his cloak.

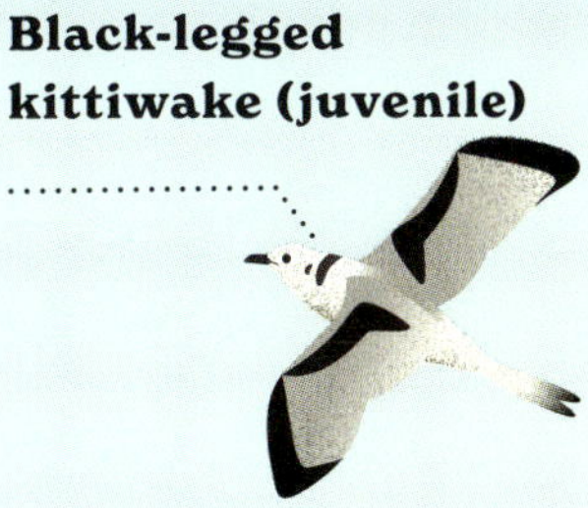

True seabirds like gannets, puffins and terns spend their lives at sea and only touch land to build nests and raise their chicks in the summer. You can often see these beautiful animals from the seashore during breeding seasons.

Geese

You might think geese are big white farm animals, but many species of wild geese visit Ireland's coast to feed in the winter. They are herbivores and like to graze in coastal fields and eelgrass meadows.

Flotsam, jetsam and beachcombing

High on the shoreline, where the highest tides drop whatever the sea was carrying, you will often find all sorts of bits and bobs.

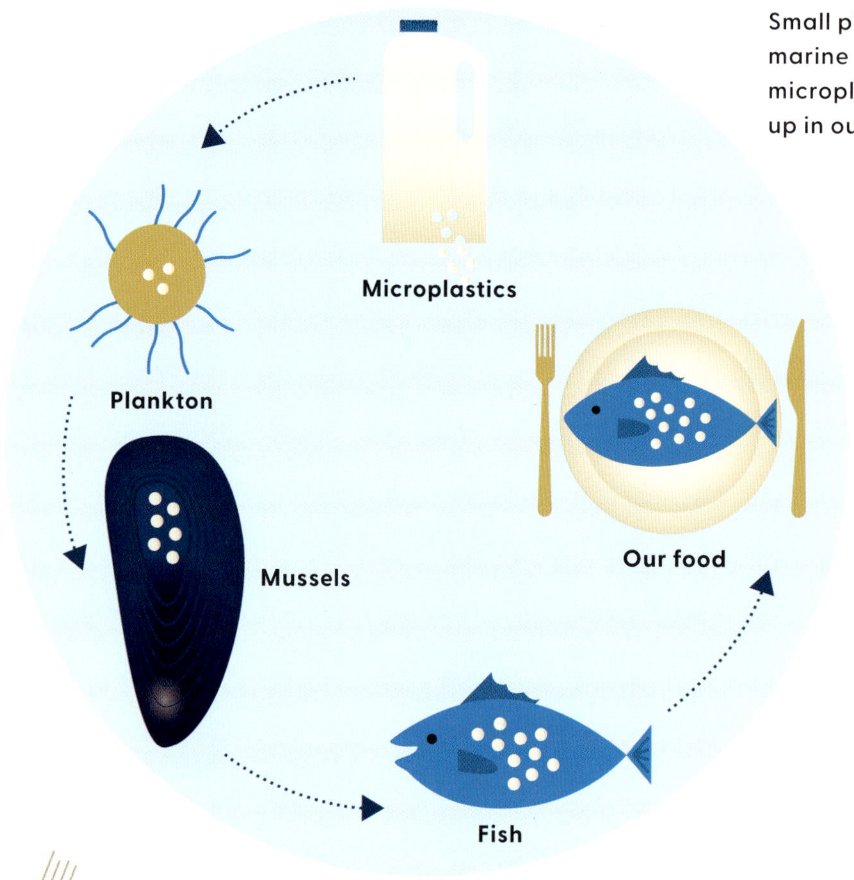

Small pieces of plastic marine litter are called microplastics. They can end up in our food.

Marine litter

Unfortunately, a lot of this is marine litter. Flotsam and jetsam are items that have ended up in the water but don't belong there. Fishing nets, ropes, fish boxes, containers and tiny bits of plastic are now common to find tangled up in seaweed and stones. The litter pollutes the water and is dangerous for marine life and for us.

Plastics

When you visit the beach, picking up multicoloured pieces of plastic and bringing them to a bin can be very satisfying, but keep your eyes peeled for little treasures! Some people collect plastic toys that have been washed up on the beach. Some litter comes from really far away or can be quite old, which shows us how the ocean connects continents, and how long it takes for plastic to biodegrade.

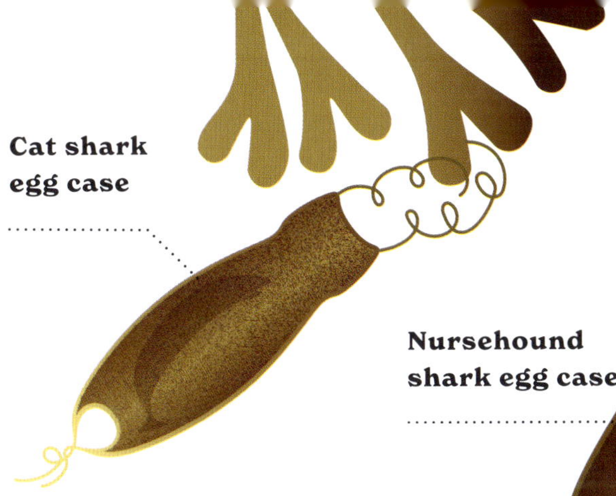

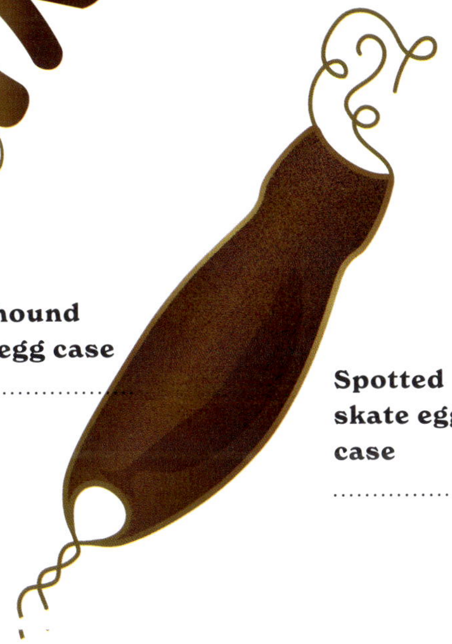

Natural treasures

Mixed with human-made items, you might find natural treasures such as sea beans or mermaid's purses. Sea beans are the pods or seeds of trees that don't grow in Ireland – they float on the surface of the ocean and may even have crossed the Atlantic Ocean from the Caribbean!

Mermaid's purses

Mermaid's purses are the egg cases of sharks and skates. They come in various shapes and sizes. If they're long and have curly tendrils, they are from one of our dogfish species, also known as cat sharks (which is a bit confusing). The curly tendrils get tangled in seaweed and hold the case in place until the tiny shark inside is ready to hatch out after about nine months.

More rectangular egg cases with straight horns coming out of each corner are from skates, which are relatives of sharks. Skates are flat and swim as if they are flying along the bottom of the sea. They have long thin tails like a whip.

Cuttlefish

You might also find a cuttlefish skeleton. Cuttlefish are related to octopus and squid. They have an internal skeleton that is made of a really light, white material that floats when the animal has died. People give these cuttlefish 'shells' to pet birds to peck at.

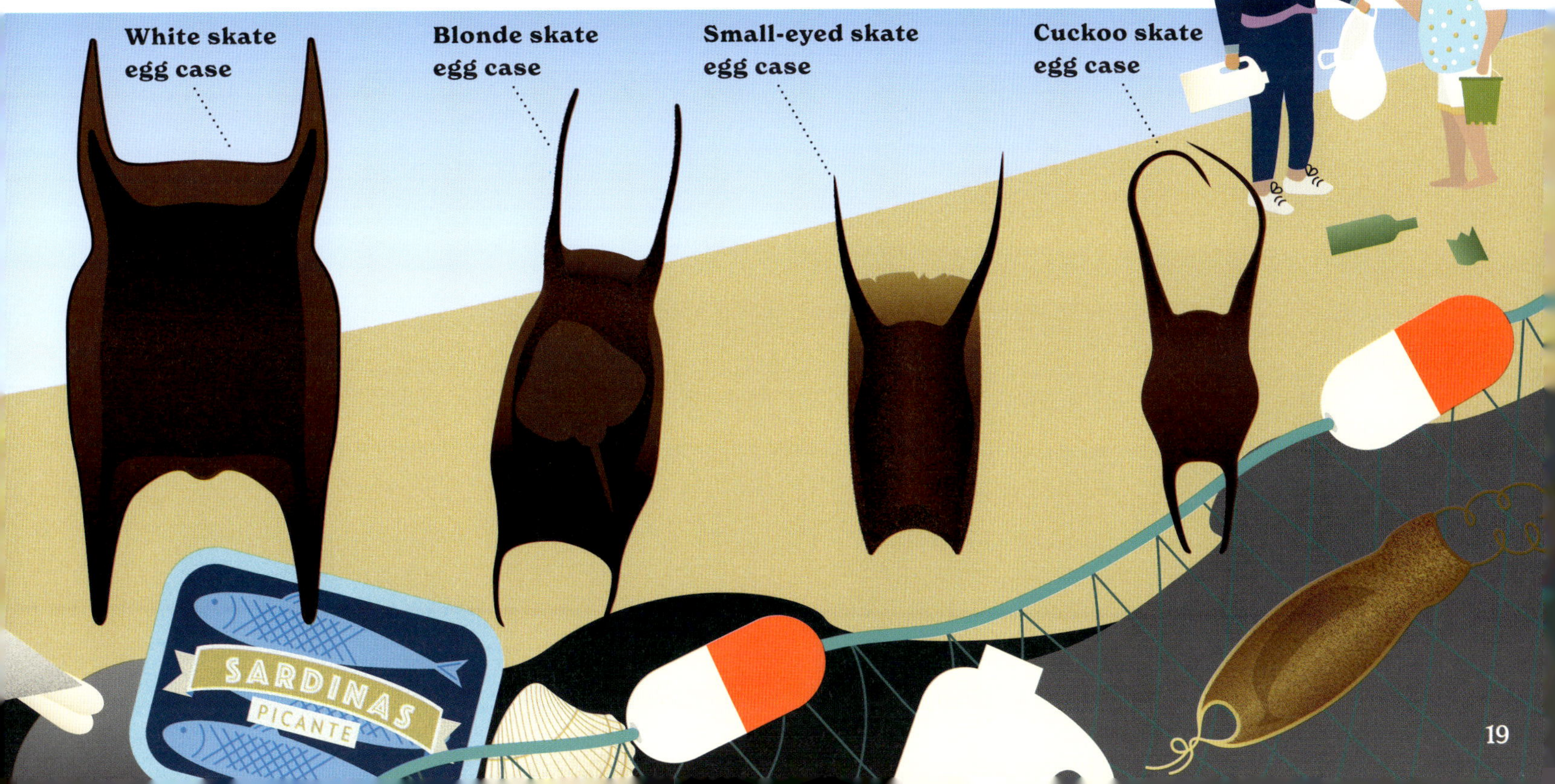

Seashore hoppers and crawlers

Seashores are full of creepy crawlers that are really important in cleaning up our shorelines.

Sand hoppers
If you've ever tried to dig in the sand to make a sandcastle on a beach, you will probably have disturbed the sand hoppers that live buried in the sand and watched them 'ping' away. Sand hoppers prefer to stay buried during the day and are usually a very similar colour to the sand.

At night, they come up to the surface and hop and crawl around gobbling up seaweed or anything else tasty that's been washed ashore. This keeps the beach clean for us! If you startle one, it can jump three metres, which is the length of a small car. That is pretty amazing, considering how small they are!

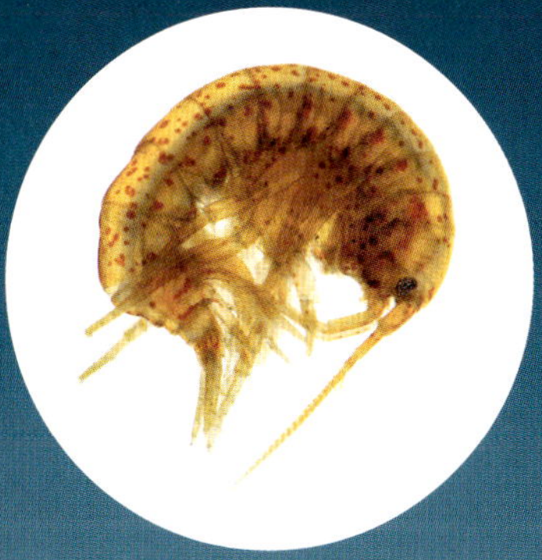

Gammarids
Further down the shoreline you might notice little creatures that look like insects under pebbles and seaweed. If they are wriggling around on their sides, they are gammarids. There are quite a few different gammarids, but you would need to be an expert with a microscope to tell them apart.

Sea slaters
Another relative of this group is the sea slater. These look like the woodlice that you might see on land. They live in cracks in piers and under stones high up on the shore where the sea rarely reaches. They come out at night-time to graze on whatever they find washed up or growing on the rocks.

These hoppers and crawlers are food for larger animals such as many of the birds that feed along our shores. It's easy for us, with our human eyes, to think they are a bit yucky, but for a bird they are delicious!

What is seaweed?

Seaweeds are really important in the web of marine life.

The seaweeds on Ireland's coast come in lots of shapes, colours and sizes – from the pink coating in rock pools to the large solid kelps that grow just below the low tide mark. Seaweed dead on the shore can be smelly and gooey, but alive in the water, seaweeds are beautiful.

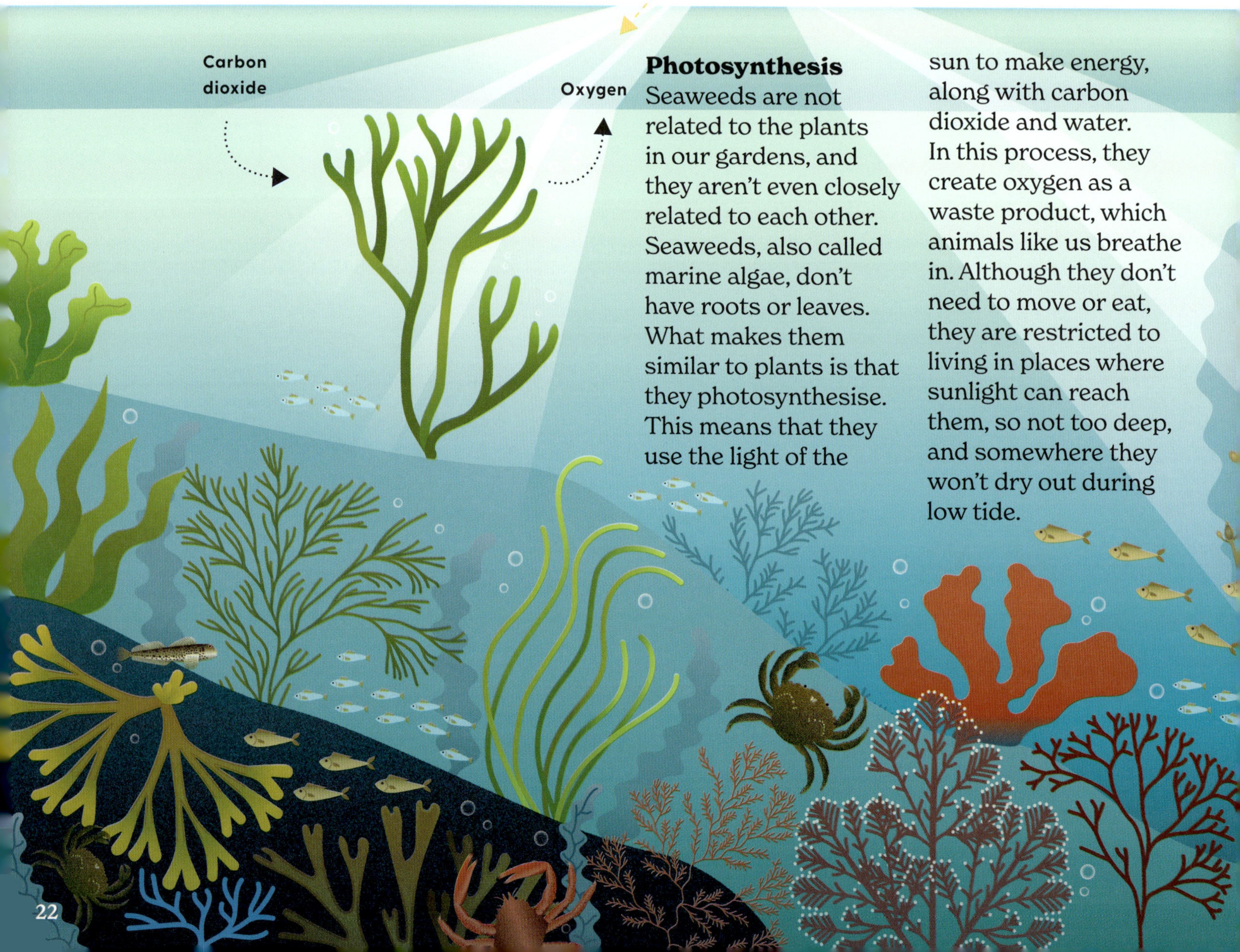

Photosynthesis

Seaweeds are not related to the plants in our gardens, and they aren't even closely related to each other. Seaweeds, also called marine algae, don't have roots or leaves. What makes them similar to plants is that they photosynthesise. This means that they use the light of the sun to make energy, along with carbon dioxide and water. In this process, they create oxygen as a waste product, which animals like us breathe in. Although they don't need to move or eat, they are restricted to living in places where sunlight can reach them, so not too deep, and somewhere they won't dry out during low tide.

Seaweed also shelters us – kelp along the coast slows down waves and reduces their power before they hit the shore, helping to reduce the impact of storms.

Many animals eat seaweeds and many more use seaweed for shelter from extreme weather and to hide from predators.

Keeping the water in balance

If there is too much nitrogen in one area of the ocean, it can upset the balance of marine life and eventually cause dead zones where there is not enough oxygen in the water for plants or animals to survive. Seaweeds absorb nutrients, including nitrogen, from the water, helping to keep everything in balance. They also create oxygen while they photosynthesise.

Why are seaweeds different colours?

To photosynthesise, seaweeds contain a chemical called chlorophyll, which plants also use. There are different types of chlorophyll, each with a different colour. These different versions of chlorophyll give seaweeds their different colours and help them to absorb light underwater. There are three main groups of seaweed: green, red and brown. As a general rule, green seaweeds are more common on the upper shore and red on the lower shore. Brown seaweeds are the most common and can be divided into groups that are found at each level on the shore.

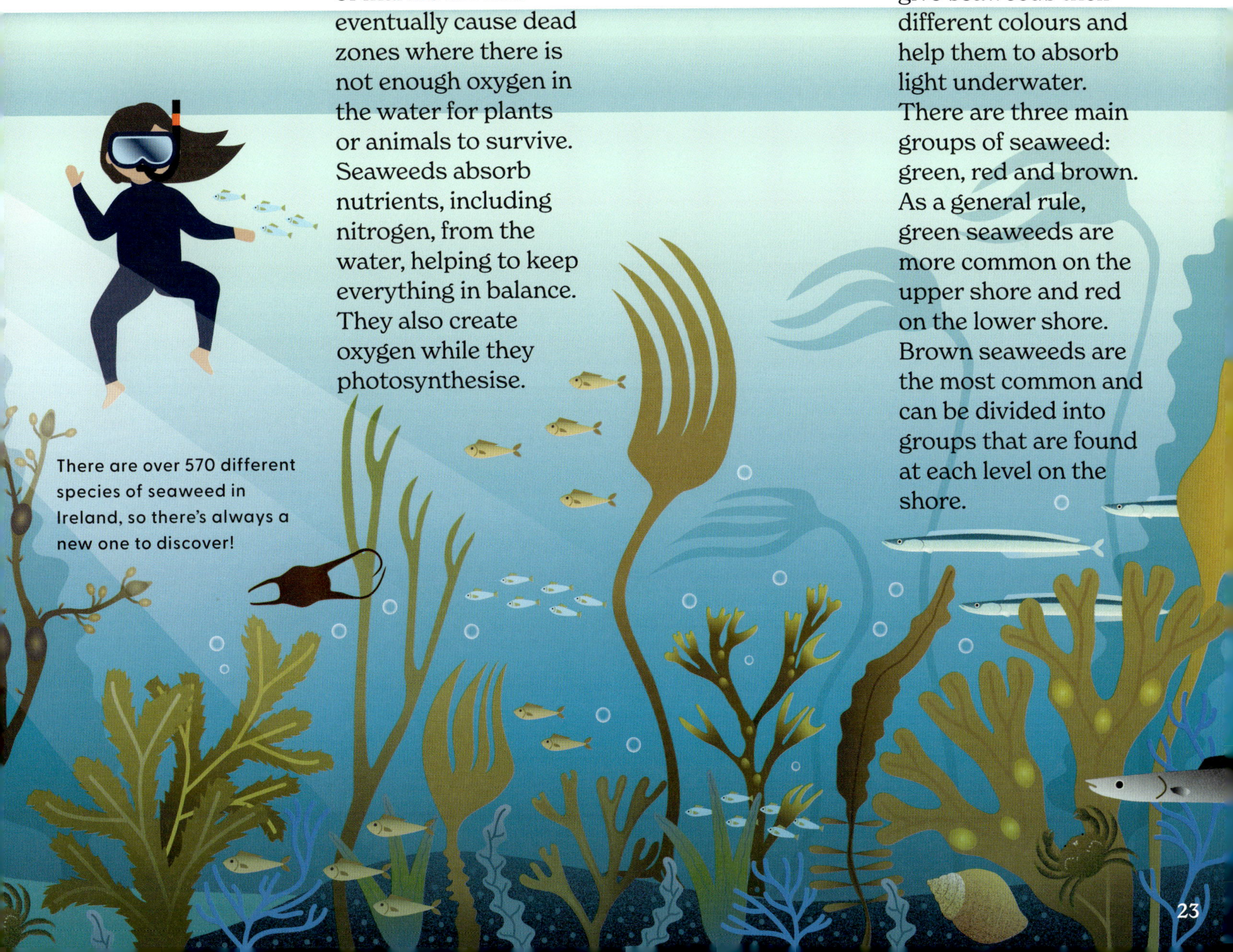

There are over 570 different species of seaweed in Ireland, so there's always a new one to discover!

Identifying seaweeds

Seaweeds look a bit different to land plants. There are many shapes, sizes and variations, but here is a guide to some of the most common seaweeds.

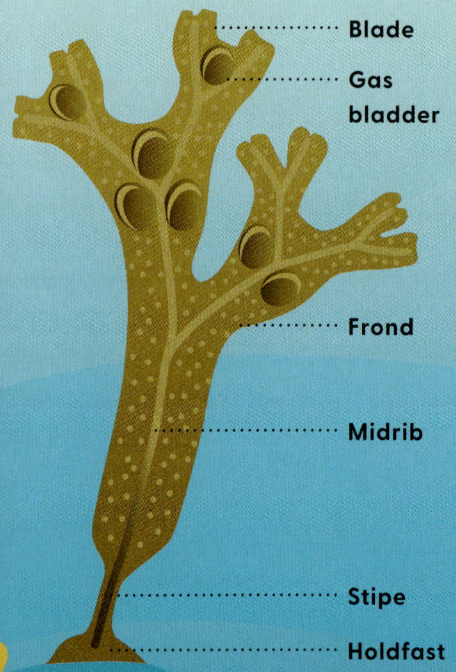

Seaweed structure
Most seaweeds cling to the seabed, a rock, or to another seaweed using a holdfast From here, many seaweeds have a stipe to hold them upright. Sometimes this stipe branches into fronds. Many seaweeds also have blades that allow the water to ripple over the seaweed. Some of the most common seaweeds on our shores have air bladders that help the fronds to float high in the water. Look on the frond for a midrib running along the centre.

Of course, there are always exceptions. You might notice hard white or pink patches coating stones, shells and even other seaweeds in rock pools. These are encrusting seaweeds. They grow across the rock and create a hard surface made of calcium.

High shore
High on the shore, look out for channelled wrack, bladder wrack, spiral wrack and horned wrack. They are all brown seaweeds that grow in small clumps and can survive being out of the water for a long time. In more sheltered places, look for sea lettuce and gutweed. These are very delicate green seaweeds.

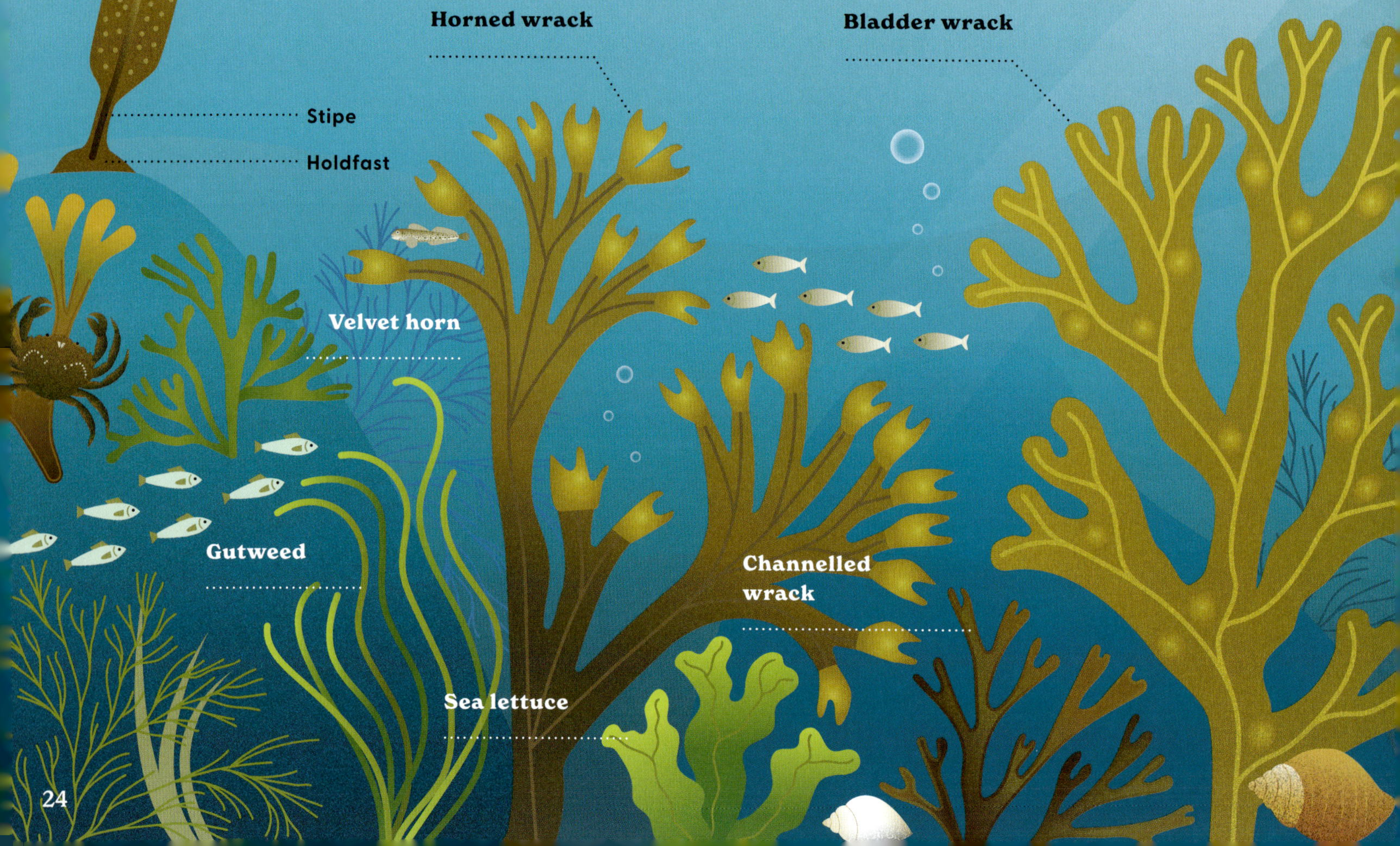

Rock pools

In rock pools, some of the most special finds are velvet horn, a green seaweed with a velvety texture, and coralline algae, which grows upright but also coats itself in a calcium shell.

Lower down the shore and in deeper rock pools, the diversity increases. Look for the delicate fronds of sea beech, carrageen and the many fragile red weeds that take cover under rocks and larger seaweeds.

Low shore

At the lowest part of the shore, at a very low tide, you might get to see some of our kelps out of the water. The two largest species are difficult to tell apart. The main difference is that oarweed has a flexible stipe, so it flops over when the tide goes out. Sugar kelp has long fronds with frilly edges.

Furbelows

Furbelows has a round bulb of a holdfast that some people call a sea hedgehog.

At low tide you might also notice seaweeds with extremely long fronds like strings. Egg wrack has large air bladders spaced out like beads on a giant necklace. Thong weed is like dark tagliatelle (that's the flat spaghetti).

Limpets, barnacles and mussels

On almost every rocky shore in Ireland, you'll find limpets, barnacles or mussels.

Lifestyles
These animals all spend their early life floating freely in the sea until they come across a good surface, usually one where there are others of their kind, and decide to drop down and settle in place. Although they have similar lifestyles and are often found in similar places, they are not at all related. Limpets are closely related to sea snails. Barnacles are related to crabs and shrimps.

Mussels are related to the other bivalves – animals that have two shells that they can separate or shut together tightly.

Barnacles
Barnacles are so numerous in some places that they can entirely cover the surface of the rocky shore with their small pointed volcano-like shells. When they decide on a place to settle, they stick their heads to the rock and build a series of shell plates around them and stay like that for the rest of their lives! When the tide comes in, each barnacle opens a tiny gap between the upper shell plates and sticks its feathery legs out into the water to catch whatever tasty morsels are passing by.

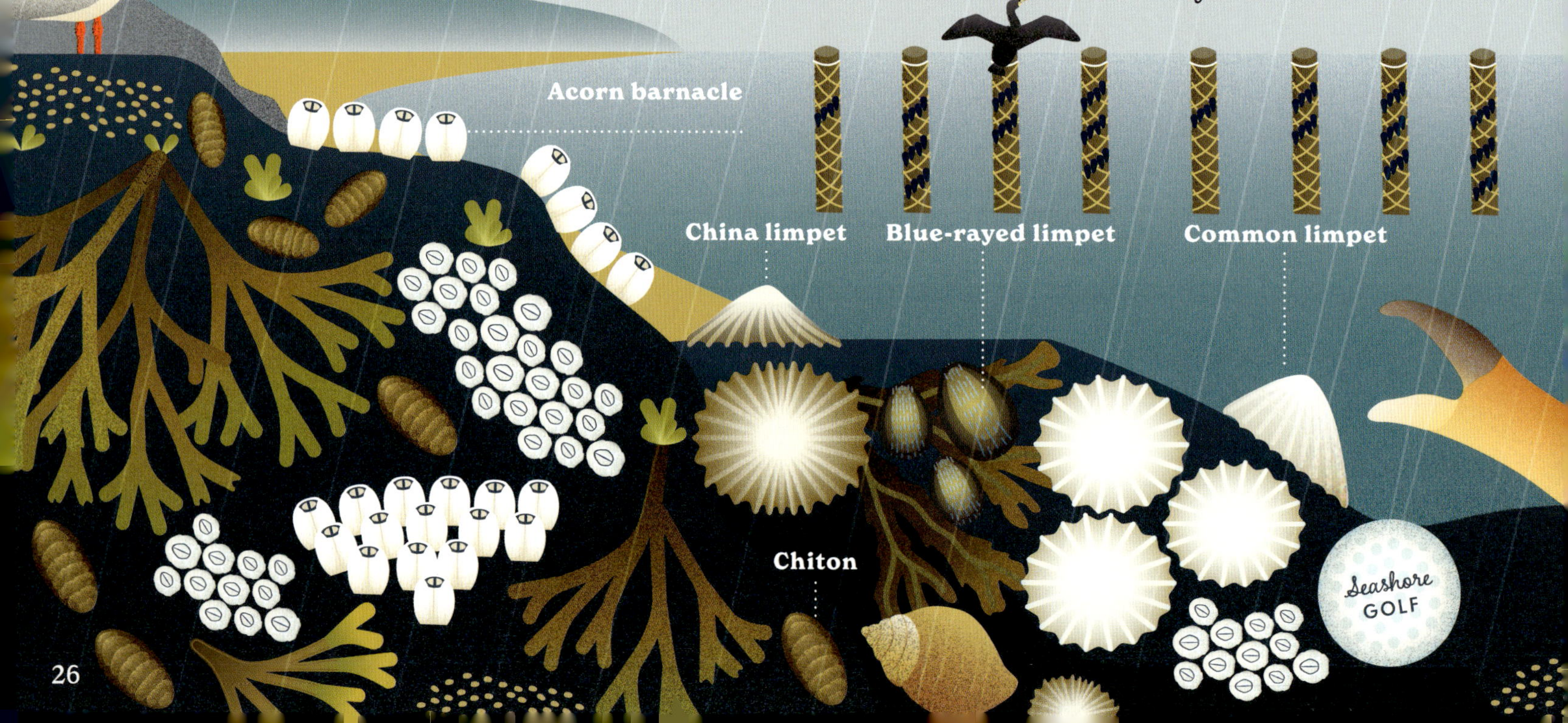

A limpet's home scar.

Barnacle

Limpets
The shells of pyramid-shaped limpets can be a similar size to a golf ball. They cling tightly to rocks when the tide is out. This stops them from getting dried out and protects them from predators. Underneath the shell is an animal with a strong foot and sharp teeth that scratch along the surface of rocks or large seaweeds, grazing on tiny particles. In some places you might even notice the marks of where limpet teeth (called radula) have scratched the rock. When the tide comes in, they loosen their grip on the rock and start to wander around looking for food. They usually return to the same spot when the tide goes out. This spot often develops a mark, or even a hollow, known as a home scar. In damp places, limpets might move around and feed when the tide is out. If you're very quiet, you might hear limpets scratching along the rock as they eat!

Mussels
Mussels don't like to be exposed to the air for long, so they live further down the shore than limpets and barnacles. Mussels use threads called byssus to attach themselves to rocks. They might detach and float around once or twice before they settle in a permanent home. Mussels are often found in dense beds. If a predator attacks the bed, the mussels can send out byssus threads, attach them to the predator and pull it off the bed.

Limpets can live for up to 17 years.

Sea snails

Far from being sticky or icky, the snails (and slugs) that live on our seashores come in many colours, shapes and sizes and are a really important part of the web of life. Here are a few of the common species you might see on Ireland's seashores.

Periwinkles
These sea snails graze in rock pools, on seaweed, and even on the shells of other animals. One you'll find quite often is the edible periwinkle, which is mostly black or dark red and as big as a garden snail. The most colourful one is the flat periwinkle, which is smaller and less pointy. Flat periwinkles can be yellow, red, green, brown or orange and they live among the seaweed on the mid shore.

Topshells
Some of the topshells, such as the toothed topshell, look quite similar to edible periwinkles. Others, such as the painted topshell, the turban topshell and the purple topshell, are much more colourful. If you turn over some types of topshell, you will notice a little 'belly button' beside the main opening on the shell.

Necklace shells and cowries

These live in the subtidal zone, but you might find their shells on the shore. Necklace shells are named after the large semi-circular structures that contain their eggs.

Whelks

Dog whelks are smaller than a garden snail but have a more pointed seashell shape. They are usually white. At low tide they often group together in crevices and you might also notice clumps of their yellow eggs in the same place. All whelks are predators and are very good at detecting their prey in the water, a bit like a dog sniffing out food. Dog whelks use a chemical to soften the shell of a barnacle or a mussel and then drill a hole using their specially adapted teeth. They then inject another chemical into the shell of the prey to stop it moving before digging in for dinner!

Slugs

Sea hares and sea lemons are just two types of sea slugs in Ireland. Sea hares are usually dark coloured and have long 'ears'. These ears are actually called rhinophores and are used to detect food and other sea hares in the water – so they work a bit more like noses than ears! In spring, they lay long strings of bright orange eggs that look a bit like tangled fishing line.

Sea lemons are usually yellow and look bumpy. They also have long rhinophores at their front end and frilly-looking gills for breathing at their back end. They mostly feed on sponges that cover rocks on the low shore and in very damp crevices on rocky shores.

Stuck in the mud

Sandy beaches, bays and estuaries might look empty, but there is often a whole array of life buried under the sand or mud. Some animals leave traces on the surface of the sand, so you'll know they're there. Others you might never notice until a storm washes an empty shell up out of the sand.

Cockles, clams and razor shells

There are many different shapes and sizes of cockles, clams, razor shells and other bivalves that live buried at different depths in the sand. Each of them has a preference for where on the shore they live, but most are found low down, close to the low tide mark or just under it. Although they vary so much, they mostly follow a similar lifestyle. They use their strong foot to dig down into the sand, where they stay while the tide comes and goes. When the tide is in, they extend their siphon up to the surface of the sand and use it like a straw to suck in water and filter out tasty particles before exhaling it out again. These siphons can become tasty treats for passing fish!

Because they are so numerous, burrowing bivalves like these are an important part of the ocean and seashore food webs. They are eaten by birds, otters, fish, crabs and people. They are also eaten by a whole host of sea snails, some of which are experts in getting into the shells of a particular bivalve species.

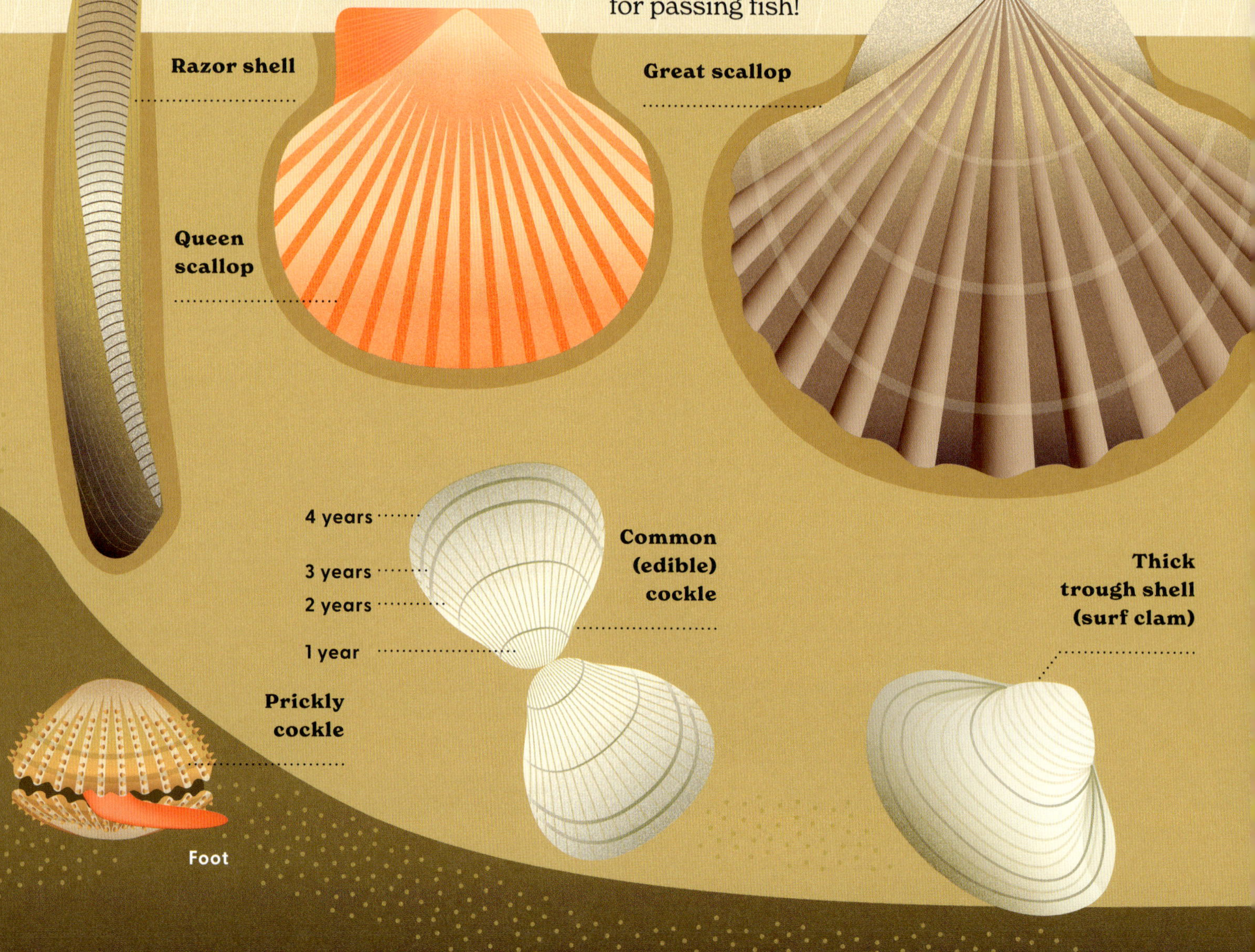

Sea potato test

The Arctic cyprine is a large bivalve that lives on sandy seafloors. Its shell has many rings that can tell scientists how old it is, just like rings in a tree. In 2006, one was found off the coast of Iceland that was 507 years old!

Sea potatoes
Sea potatoes or heart urchins (people call them different things) look a bit like a spiny mouse when they're alive. When they die, the short brown spines fall out and just the very delicate, heart-shaped urchin test (shell) remains. They live just underneath the sand and use their tubed feet to pick up small particles that have sunk down into the sand.

Underground predators
Masked crabs are the only crabs in Ireland to live underground. They burrow into the sand using their back legs and then hold their extremely long antennae up to the surface, leaving a small gap between them. They pull water down this gap so that they can breathe (similar to how we use a snorkel). They feed on other small animals buried under the sand.

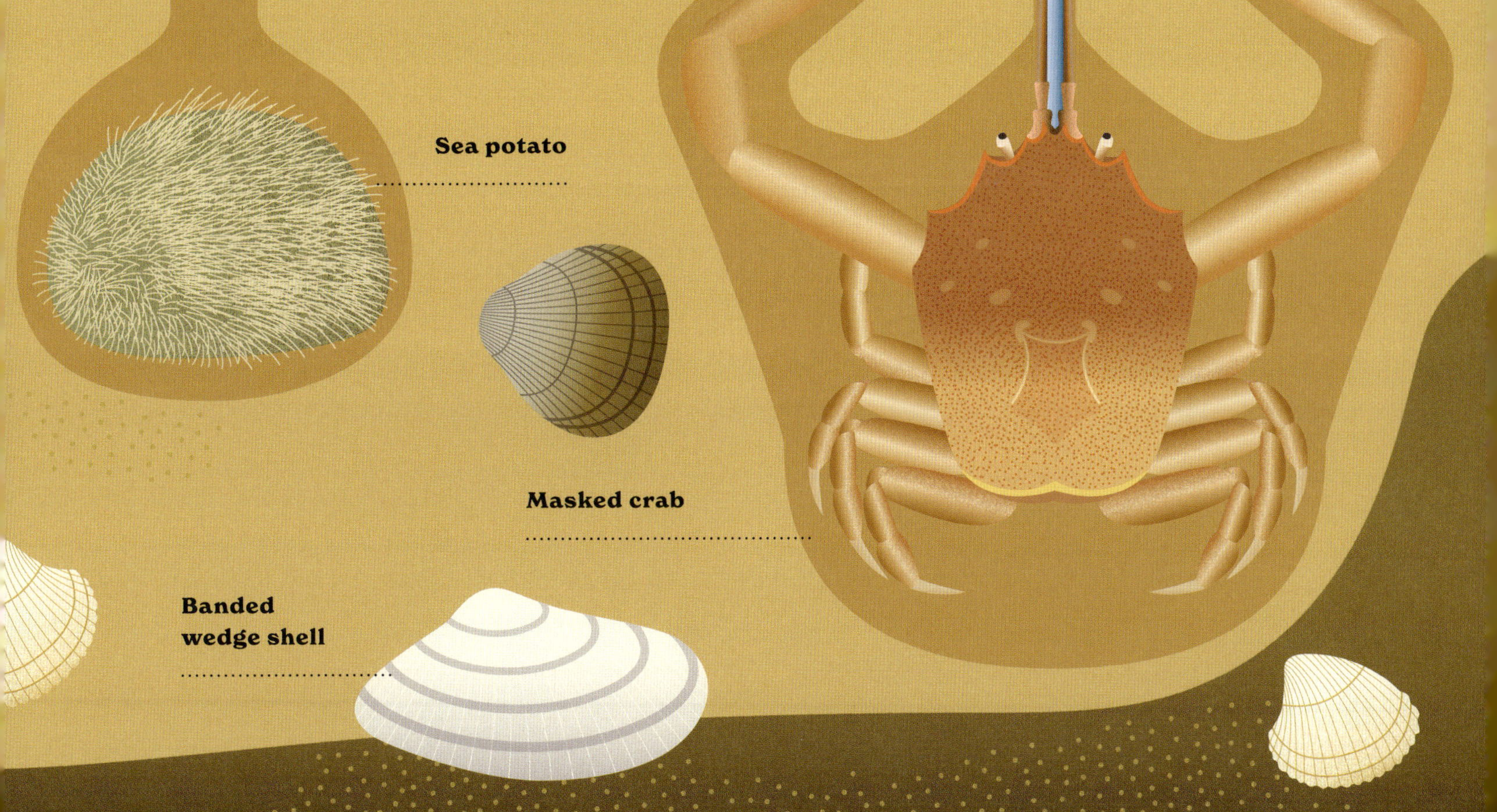

Anemones

Sea anemones are relatives of jellyfish. They have stinging tentacles that surround their mouth and wave in the water to find food.

How do they eat?
Although they mostly eat very small animals, you might catch an anemone in the act of eating a jellyfish, fish or even crabs much bigger than them. As well as their external tentacles, some anemones have internal tentacles that they use to control wriggling prey once they have caught it and ingested it.

Stings
Anemones are very careful about when they trigger their stinging cells. They are selective because each sting can only fire once and then it needs to be replaced, which takes a lot of energy. They are also careful not to sting themselves! Some animals have developed ways to live within anemone tentacles.

Tiny beadlet anemone babies live inside the parent's body column until they are ready to emerge out of the mouth of the adult and find their own place to live.

Beadlet anemones

Beadlet anemones are very common on Irish seashores. They are usually dark red but can be green. When the tide is out, they look like jelly blobs stuck to the rocks because they curl their tentacles and their mouth inside their body column to protect themselves. In rock pools or when the tide comes back in, you might see their sturdy tentacles emerge. They have a ring of bright blue 'beads' behind their tentacles that also contain stinging cells. These can be used to attack other anemones if there is too much competition for space or food. Strawberry anemones look similar but have bright green spots on their column.

Snakelocks anemones

Snakelocks anemones can't retract their very long tentacles, so prefer to live further down the shore where they are rarely dry at low tide. Snakelocks anemones are grey or beige, but they sometimes absorb brightly coloured algae into their bodies that turn them bright purple and green like tropical corals. The algae and the anemone help each other to survive. This is called a symbiotic relationship.

Anemones are not always the predator – they are also eaten by sea slugs.

Other anemones

You might find wartlet or gem anemones (same thing, different names) in rock pools. These grape-sized anemones often live in groups. They have striped white-and-green tentacles. If they are threatened, they retract their tentacles into their body column, which is covered in wart-like bumps and looks like a little sea urchin.

Crabs and shrimps

Prawns, shrimps, lobsters and crabs are all part of the same family – the decapods.

Ten feet

Decapod means 'ten feet' because they have five pairs of legs. The front pair often has large claws. Sometimes the other legs have much smaller pincers as well.

Decapod bodies and legs are covered by a tough exoskeleton, which is like a shell but doesn't grow in size. When the animal inside grows, it needs to drop its shell. This is called moulting. After a crab moults, it has no protection and must hide away until its new shell hardens. It must feel quite scared!

Hermit crabs

Hermit crabs have a different lifestyle – they don't have a shell on most of their body and instead live inside the empty shells of other animals. When they outgrow their shell, they examine bigger shells very carefully until they find one that is a good fit and then they quickly jump into it and get settled. On the seashore, the shells of dog whelks and periwinkles provide perfect accommodation for hermit crabs.

A *gliomóg* is a small lobster in Irish, which is quite similar to *liomóg* – the pinch that a lobster might give you! Lobsters can live for a very long time – sometimes as long as 75 years.

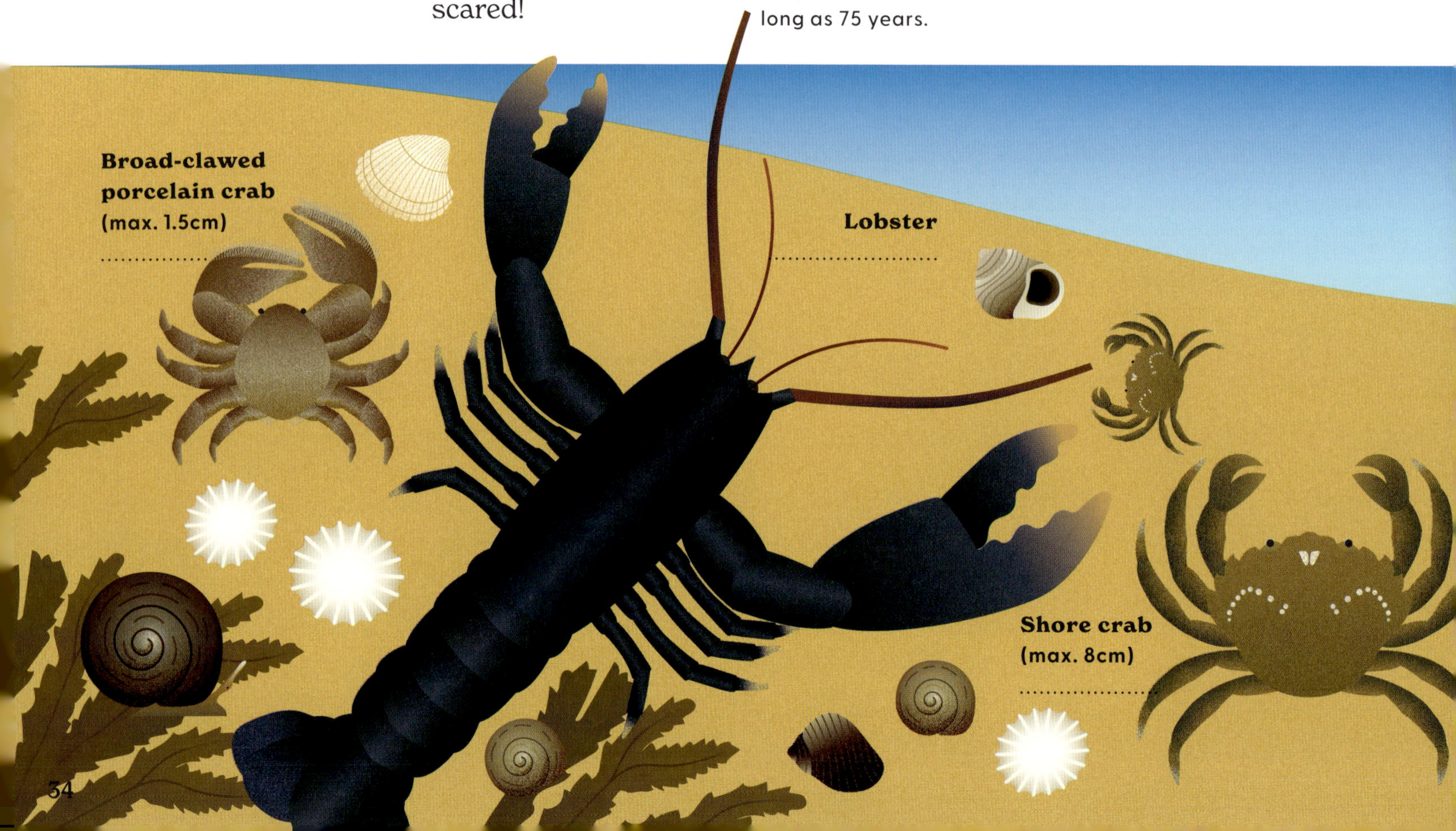

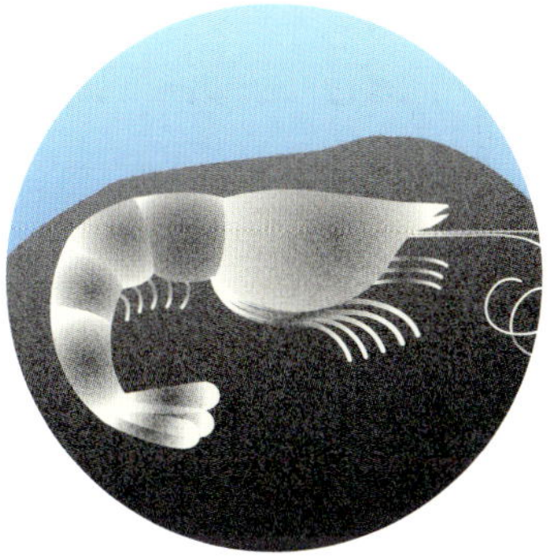

Shrimps

Shrimp exoskeletons are nearly see-through when they're alive, so shrimps can be tricky to find in rock pools. If you sit very still, you might notice a curious one coming out to take a look at you or pick up something tasty to eat. Unlike crabs, shrimps can swim through the water using their tails. Some crabs do have flattened back legs that they use like paddles to swim short distances, but their heavy shells and wide bodies keep them mostly on the ground.

Baby shellfish

Sometimes you might notice tiny dark or brightly coloured eggs attached to the underside of a crab. This means you have found a berried female who is caring for her eggs until they hatch out to float with other plankton. It's important to leave these females alone to give the eggs the best chance of survival. Some crabs take many years to reach their maximum size.

There are quite a few different crab species you might see on the shore – some are tiny and could sit on your finger, while others might be as wide as an adult's hand.

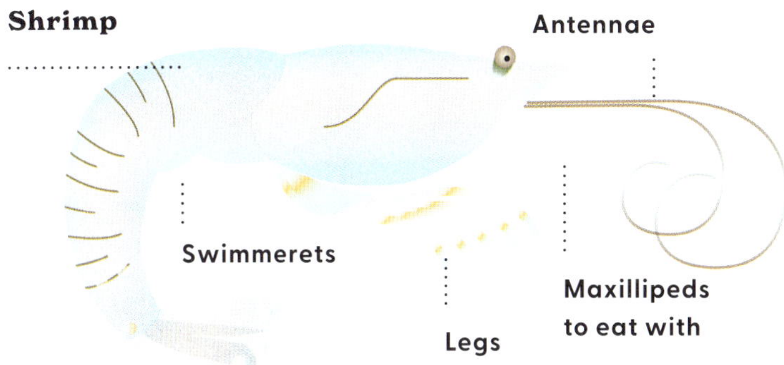

Sea squirts and sponges

Low down on the shore you might find sea squirts and sponges. These other-worldly creatures have similar lifestyles, but are not closely related at all.

Sponges
It's amazing to imagine that sponges are animals, but they are some of the first animals that appeared on earth. A sponge can regrow from small fragments if its body is broken up. Many of them also develop symbiotic relationships with other species, which is basically teamwork. For example, the sponge provides a safe place for the tiny algae to live and in return, the algae create extra food for the sponge. Sponges might also grow on scallops, which camouflages the scallops and protects them from predators – while also helping the sponges, because scallops are more powerful and can pull more food particles towards them.

Encrusting sponges
Under large rocks or in damp crevices on rocky shores, you might notice an orange or green patch covering the rock. The texture might be smooth and glossy like icing, or bumpier and more irregular, but there will be many little holes – these are encrusting sponges. The holes are the ostia and the oscula, which are where water flows in and out of the sponge. Inside the body, tiny hairs move the water around and filter out food particles. These sponges have no fixed body shape.

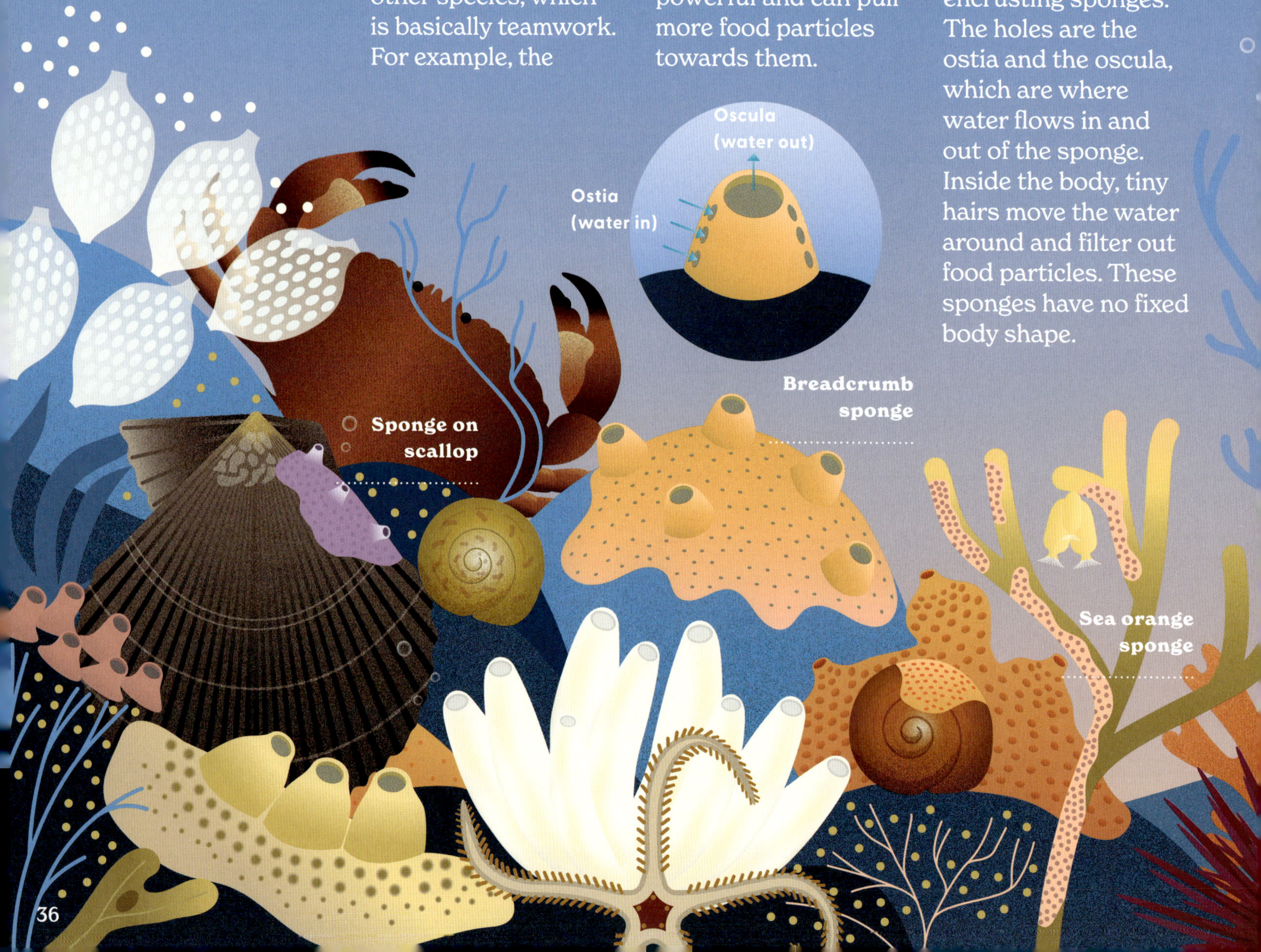

Boring sponges
Boring sponges sound like they're no fun. Actually, the word 'boring' here refers to their habit of boring holes into stone or shells. They make a tiny hole in the surface and then continue to develop a network of cavities a bit like a rabbit's den inside the stone.

Sea squirts
Adult sea squirts seem quite similar to sponges – they pump water in and out of their bodies, filtering out small food particles. Most live as individual animals attached to rocks or other hard surfaces. Some form colonies that cover rocks, but they are more organised and regular-shaped than sponges. Squirts that float in the water as adults, not attached to anything, are called salps. You might find these washed ashore after storms.

Early in their life cycle, all sea squirts have a larval stage where they look very similar to a tadpole. During this stage they have tails, eyes, brains and a nerve cord a bit like our spines.

Purse sponges look like small white leaves hanging from rocks or seaweeds.

Worms

Seashore worms usually stay well hidden under the sand or in crevices but, just like our garden worms, they are an important part of the overall web of life.

Lugworms

The most obvious worm on the seashore is the lugworm. Lugworms live in J-shaped burrows beneath wet sand. When they make these burrows, they create twisted piles of sand called casts on the surface, which you may have noticed on the beach. Lugworms filter the sand searching for particles to eat in a similar way to earthworms. Females lay eggs in their burrows, where the tiny larvae develop for the first stage of their lives.

Ragworms

Ragworms are more showy. They come in a range of colours – pink, red, green, purple – and are often shiny. They also live in burrows but you might see them on the sand or pebbles, crawling around and feeding.

Green-leaf worms

The green-leaf worm lives in rocky crevices. It moves quickly and you might see it among barnacles, which it likes to eat if their shells become damaged. In the springtime you might notice green jelly-blobs that look a bit like small grapes among the seaweed in rock pools. We think that these are the eggs of the green-leaf worm, but we don't know for sure.

Tube worms

Many worms create tubes to live in. These tubes are perfect for their soft bodies. Spiral worms create tiny coiled tubes on rocks or seaweed. Honeycomb worms are less common, as they like warmer water. Each worm builds its own tube of sand, but they live in colonies of many of these tubes attached to each other. These are honeycomb worm reefs. Peacock worms and sand masons create individual tubes within the sand. You may only notice the very tip of these tubes during a very low tide. All of these worms have feathery or frilly parts on their heads that they can stick out of their tubes to catch food.

Bootlace worms

The longest worm on the seashore is the bootlace worm, which can grow up to 10 metres long. That's nearly as long as a bus! When it's disturbed, it produces mucus that makes it slippery and hard to catch. You'll normally only see them curled up in a tangled mass on the very low shore in places where there is muddy sand. They are so long that they can tie themselves into a knot.

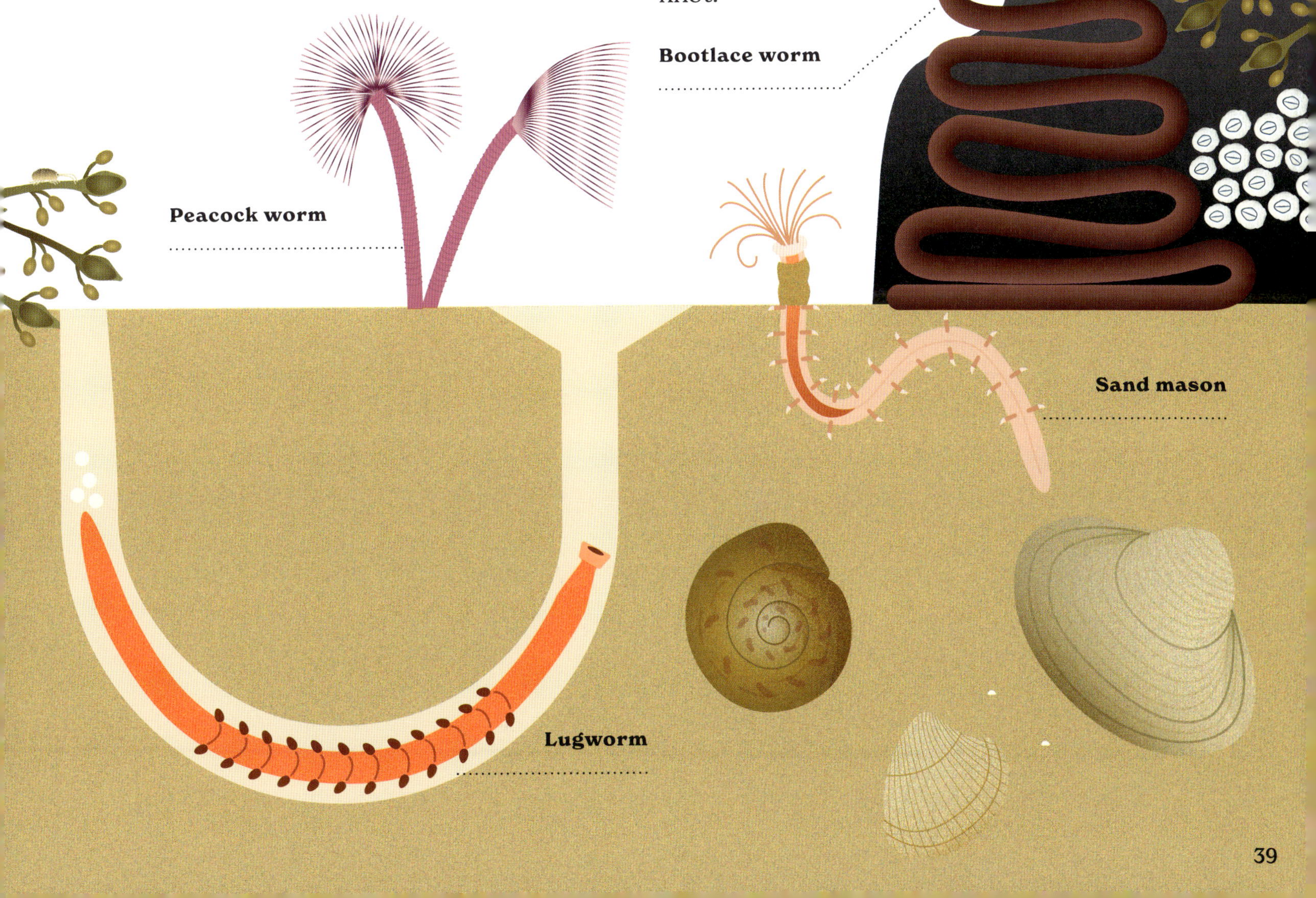

Starfish and urchins

At first glance, you might not think that starfish and urchins have anything in common. In fact, they are closely related to each other.

Spiny skin
Starfish and urchins are part of a group of animals called Echinodermata, which comes from the Greek for spiny skin. There are lots of animals in this group, but we'll look at some of the ones you're most likely to see on Irish seashores.

Symmetry
Most animals, including us, have bilateral symmetry. This means that our left side is a mirror image of our right side, and the other way around. Echinoderms are completely different. They have five-rayed symmetry. This means that instead of having a left and a right side, they have five sides laid out in a circle. This is really obvious in the starfish that have five arms, and when you look at a complete urchin from above.

Hard plates
Echinoderms also have hard plates that give their bodies structure. In starfish, these plates are internal. In urchins, they are stuck together to make the test, which is what an urchin shell is called.

The Irish for sea urchin is *gráinneog thrá*, which means 'beach hedgehog'!

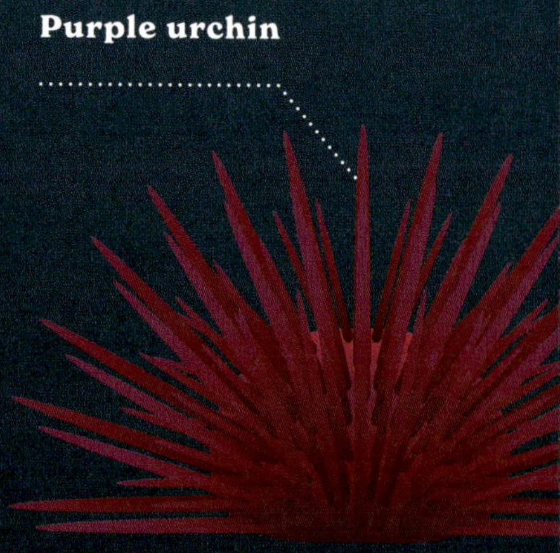

Superpowers

Starfish have the amazing ability to regrow their legs if one is broken (or bitten) off. You might notice a starfish with one leg much shorter than the others – this short one is in the process of regrowing. Their legs are very powerful and some starfish are predators. They use their legs to pull apart shells of mussels and other animals. But there isn't much space for food inside a starfish, so they pop their stomach out of their mouth to partially digest the mussel until it is soft enough for the starfish to pull the stomach back into its body to finish off digestion.

Tube feet

Another amazing thing that starfish and urchins have in common is their tube feet. They are not just for getting the starfish or urchin from one place to the next – they also grab food items and push them towards the mouth, which is at the centre of the underside. Some of the tube feet on urchins have tiny pincers for grabbing. Urchins also use them to pick up bits of shell or seaweed to use as camouflage to protect them from the sun and from predators.

This is all pretty amazing for a group of animals that don't have brains!

Cushion stars

Fish

We're getting close to the end of the encyclopedia and we still haven't mentioned fish!

Seashore fish
Many fish move in over the shore to feed when the tide comes in, but there are a few that live most of their lives close to the shore. These fish have some special features that help them to live among waves, constant motion, and the ever-changing temperatures of the shore.

Smooth skin
Seashore fish don't usually have scales on their skin and some of them have extremely smooth skin. This probably helps them to slide along the seashore and move between stones and pebbles easily. Butterfish live between pebbles and in rock pools. They are extremely difficult to pick up because they're so slithery, which probably also helps them to escape from predators.

Swim bladder
Most fish have an organ in their bodies called a swim bladder, which helps them to float and move up and down in the water. This is smaller in some seashore fish, or even missing. This helps them to stay down on the sea floor rather than being tossed about in waves.

Some seashore fish like the butterfish have developed gills that let them breathe air when the tide goes out. They still need to stay damp and cool, though.

Standing still

Many shore fish have developed ways to stand still or cling to hard surfaces. The clingfish has a sucker on its underside that can grip stones. The shore clingfish also has bright blue spots (like eyes) on the top of its head behind its real eyes that make it look like it's wearing glasses!

Rock pool fish

Shannies and blennies are common rock pool fish. They swim around looking for food when the tide is in. When it starts to go out, they often return to their favourite rock pool, where they rest until the tide comes back in again. They are extremely fast, though, so often you'll only know they're in a rock pool because you notice a flash of action as soon as they detect you peering in!

One seashore fish to watch out for is the weever fish. These predators hide just underneath the sand with their eyes and upper fins visible. These fins contain venom that can cause a painful sting if you accidentally stand on one.

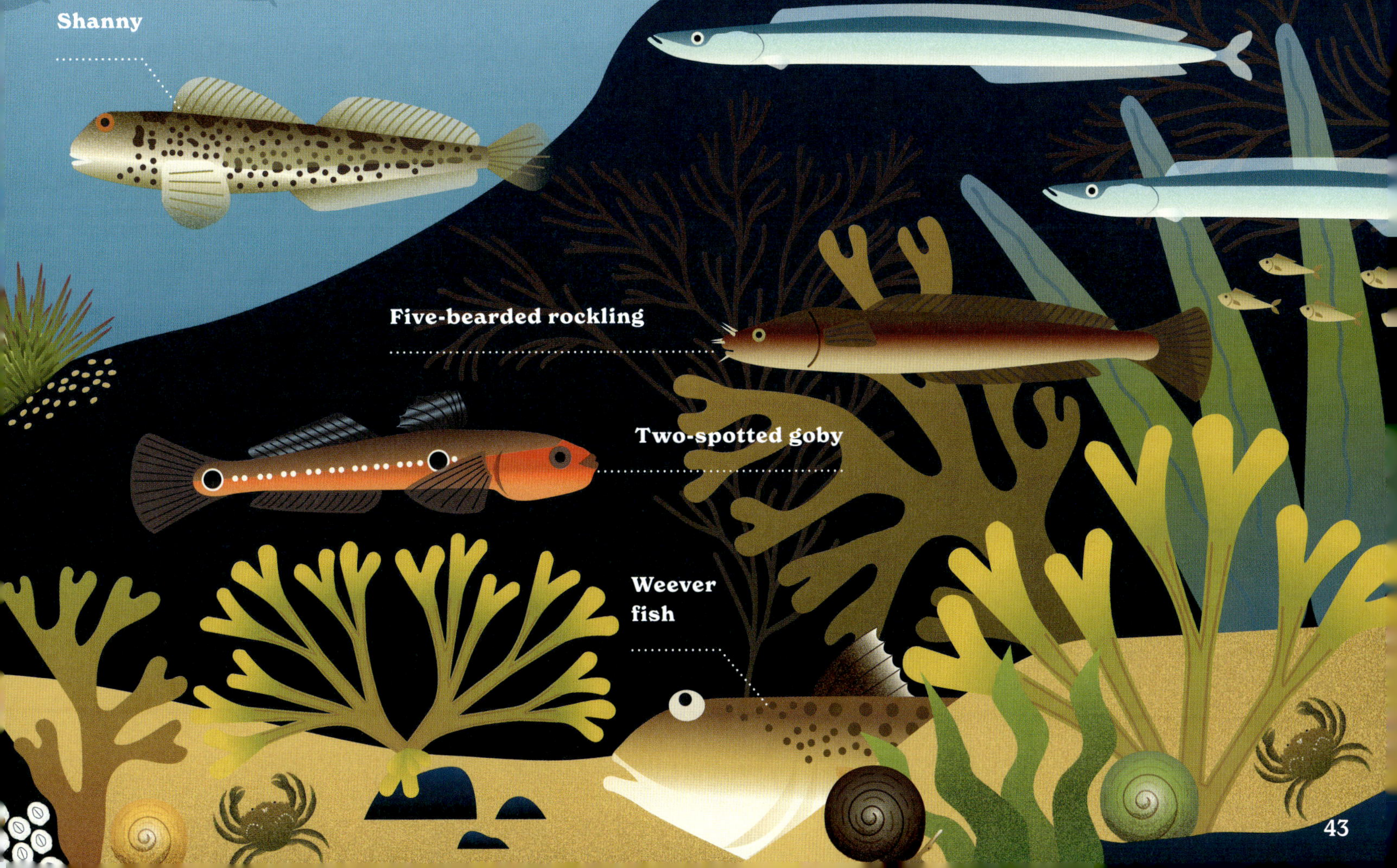

Underwater reefs and seagrass

Some important plants and animals create hard structures and places for other sea creatures to shelter, called reefs.

Coral beaches

If you're very lucky, you might have visited one of Ireland's coral beaches. Instead of sand, these beaches are covered in tiny broken pieces of what looks like tropical coral. In fact, they are a type of red coralline algae that has a calcium skeleton. This seaweed, called maërl, is pink or red when it's alive and bleaches white on the shore. It creates beds (also called reefs) on the sea floor where other plants and animals live.

Red coralline algae

Coral beach

Reefs

Animals can create underwater reefs as well. Horse mussels are similar to the blue mussels you might see attached to a rock, but they often live on sandy seabeds, where they clump together to form vast beds. Our native oyster is also a reef-forming species, but it has become quite rare. These reefs are like an oasis in the sandy seabed desert. They are below the low tide mark but, if there is a reef nearby, you might find lots of oyster shells or horse mussel shells washed up on the beach or shoreline.

In winter, geese fly south from their summer homes farther north and graze on eelgrass.

Seagrass

Ireland has two different species of seagrass, also called eelgrass. One of these grows below the low tide mark. The other grows up to the mid shore on flat sandy bays where the sand is very fine, so it doesn't dry out completely when the tide is out.

Seagrass is quite rare in Ireland now, but it is important for many reasons. Some animals eat seagrass, but many more hide among the blades of grass. The roots tunnel down under the surface where they hold the sand together and protect the shore from waves. This also creates a safe place for animals such as cockles to burrow and live.

Horse mussels

The spiny seahorse and short-snouted seahorse shelter in seagrass beds.

Jellyfish

Jellyfish aren't fish at all – they are more closely related to sea anemones.

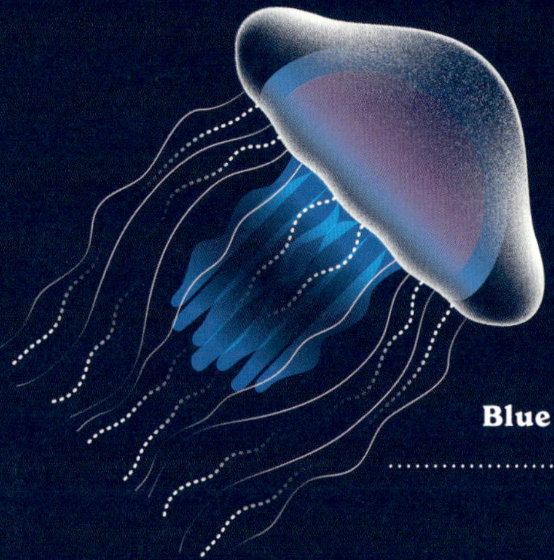

Blue jellyfish

Jellyfish life cycles

Jellyfish have complex life cycles that can involve different stages, including a microscopic stage, a phase where they are attached to a hard surface, and the main adult phase. Jellyfish don't have brains or blood, but they do have nerves on their bells (the main body part) that help them to sense light and to keep their balance in the water so they know if they're going up or down. They absorb oxygen from the water through their skin.

Here are some of the jellyfish you might find washed ashore or floating close to the shore in Ireland.

Tentacles

Jellyfish have stinging tentacles, but that doesn't mean that we should hate them. Some jellies can't sting human skin, many jellies are quite beautiful when they swim through the water, and all jellies are an important part of the web of life in the ocean. Jellyfish are eaten by leatherback turtles, seabirds, anemones and each other! They use their stinging tentacles and their feeding arms to capture prey and move it towards their mouth.

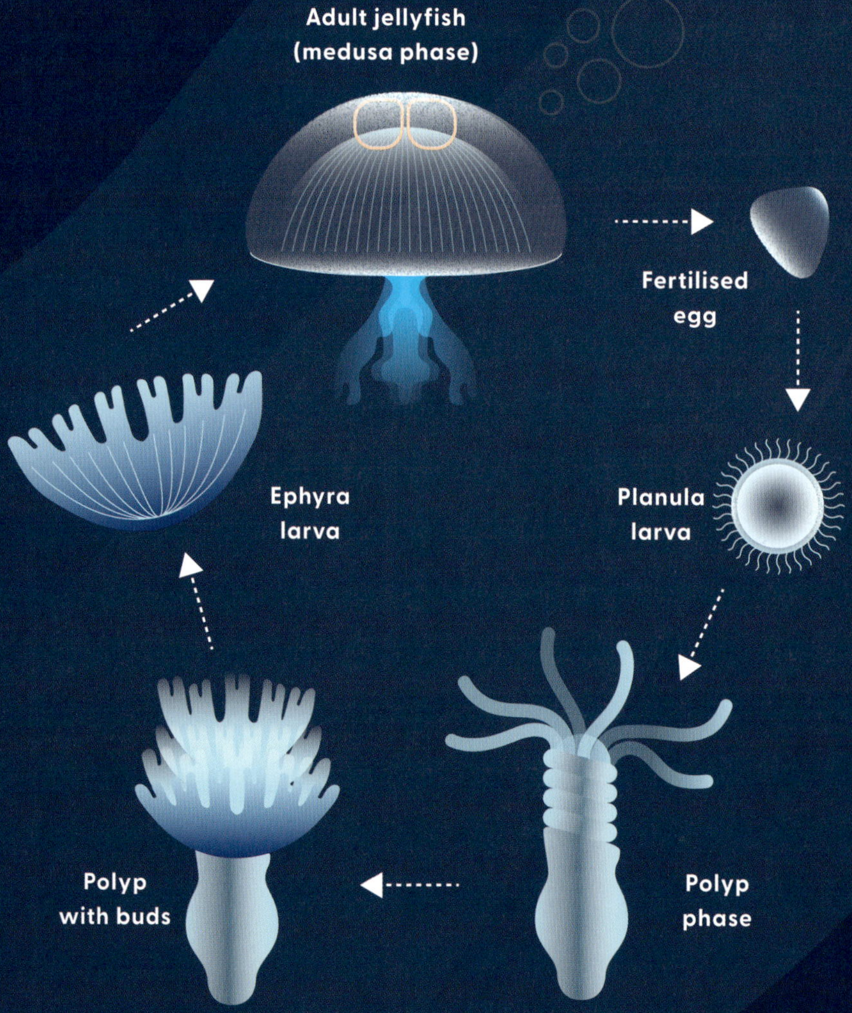

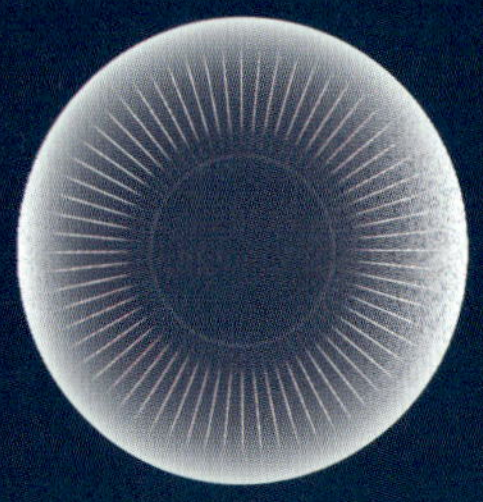

Moon jellyfish

Compass jellyfish

In Irish, these jellyfish are called *smugairle róin*, which means 'seal snot'!

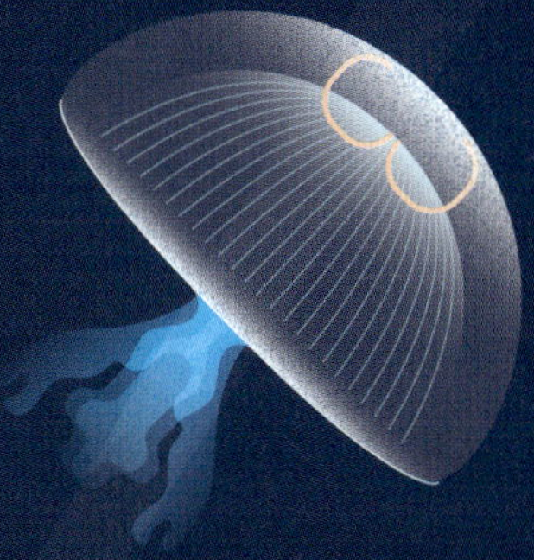

Lion's mane jellyfish
These are the biggest and most feared jellyfish in Ireland. They are more common in the Irish Sea than in the Atlantic. The bell of a lion's mane jellyfish could be wider than a car. They have a very painful sting.

Compass jellyfish
Also quite common, the compass jellyfish has brown markings on its bell and long frilly arms. Its tentacles can sting. People who have been stung compare it to a nettle sting.

Mauve stinger

Moon jellyfish
This is the most common jellyfish in Irish water. They can appear in large blooms in the summer. Thankfully, they can't sting human skin. They have a transparent bell with four pink or purple C-shaped structures. Their tentacles are very fine and there are four 'arms' surrounding the mouth that are also transparent.

Barrel jellyfish

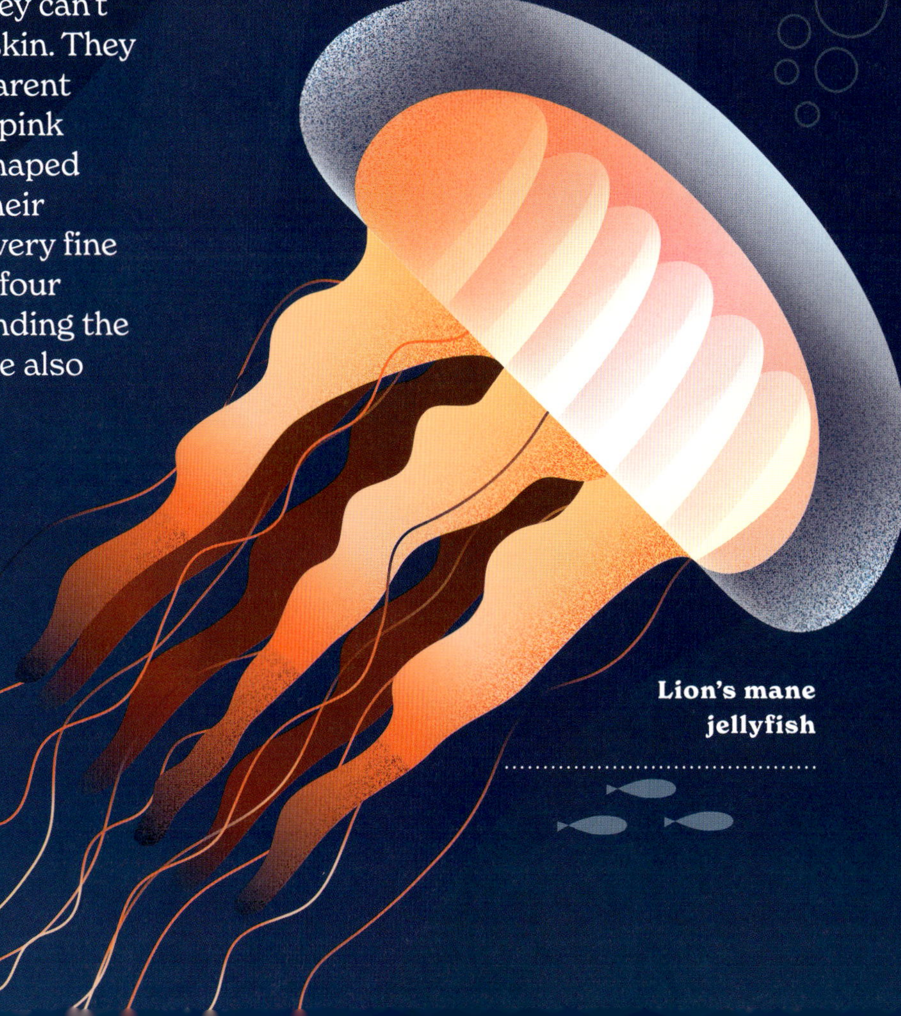

Lion's mane jellyfish

Other ocean drifters

These are some other animals that spend their lives travelling on ocean currents or being blown along the ocean surface by the wind.

Jelly-ish animals

Relatives of jellyfish, these are actually collections of tiny animals that organise themselves into a shape that looks like one big animal.

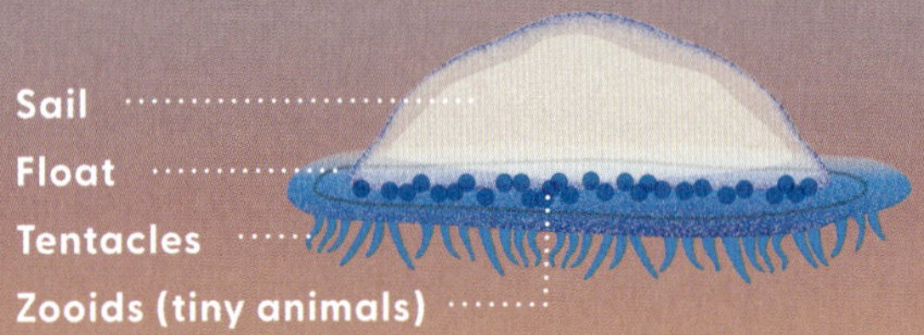

Portuguese man o' war

The Portuguese man o' war has a blue balloon-like float (called a pneumatophore) that sits on the surface of the water. Long blue tentacles trail for a few metres below. These tentacles have cells called nematocysts that contain a tiny pointed tube that can inject venom strong enough to kill a small fish. This venom is painful and can damage human skin, so avoid touching them, even when they've washed ashore.

Amazingly, some fish can live among the tentacles of Portuguese men o' war, and some animals, including turtles, sunfish and the violet snail, eat them. To avoid dangers on the surface, Portuguese men o' war can deflate their floats and sink. They also have some control of the pink-edged sail along the top of their pneumatophore.

By-the-wind sailors
By-the-wind-sailors are related to Portuguese men o' war, but they are not dangerous to humans. They look like small plastic discs. When they're alive, this disc sits on the surface of the water and has a small sail running diagonally across it that is blown by the wind. Small blue tentacles dangle into the water to catch microscopic animals. The direction of the sail is fixed on each by-the-wind-sailor and determines how it will be blown in the wind.

Violet snails
We always think of snails as creatures that crawl, but did you know that there are some that hang upside down at the surface of the ocean? Violet snails create little bubble rafts that keep them afloat as they drift around hoping that the wind will bring them in contact with by-the-wind-sailors and similar animals for them to eat! Their shells are very thin and fragile, but you might find them on the shore after strong winds.

Goose barnacles
These are relatives of the tiny barnacles that cover our rocky shores, but they prefer to travel the ocean. They attach themselves to floating timber, plastic, boats, or any other solid surface in the sea. They have long necks and five white shell plates. Feathery legs emerge from these shells to trap tiny particles of food when the barnacle is underwater. Goose barnacles have similar colouring to barnacle geese and people used to believe that they were young barnacle geese!

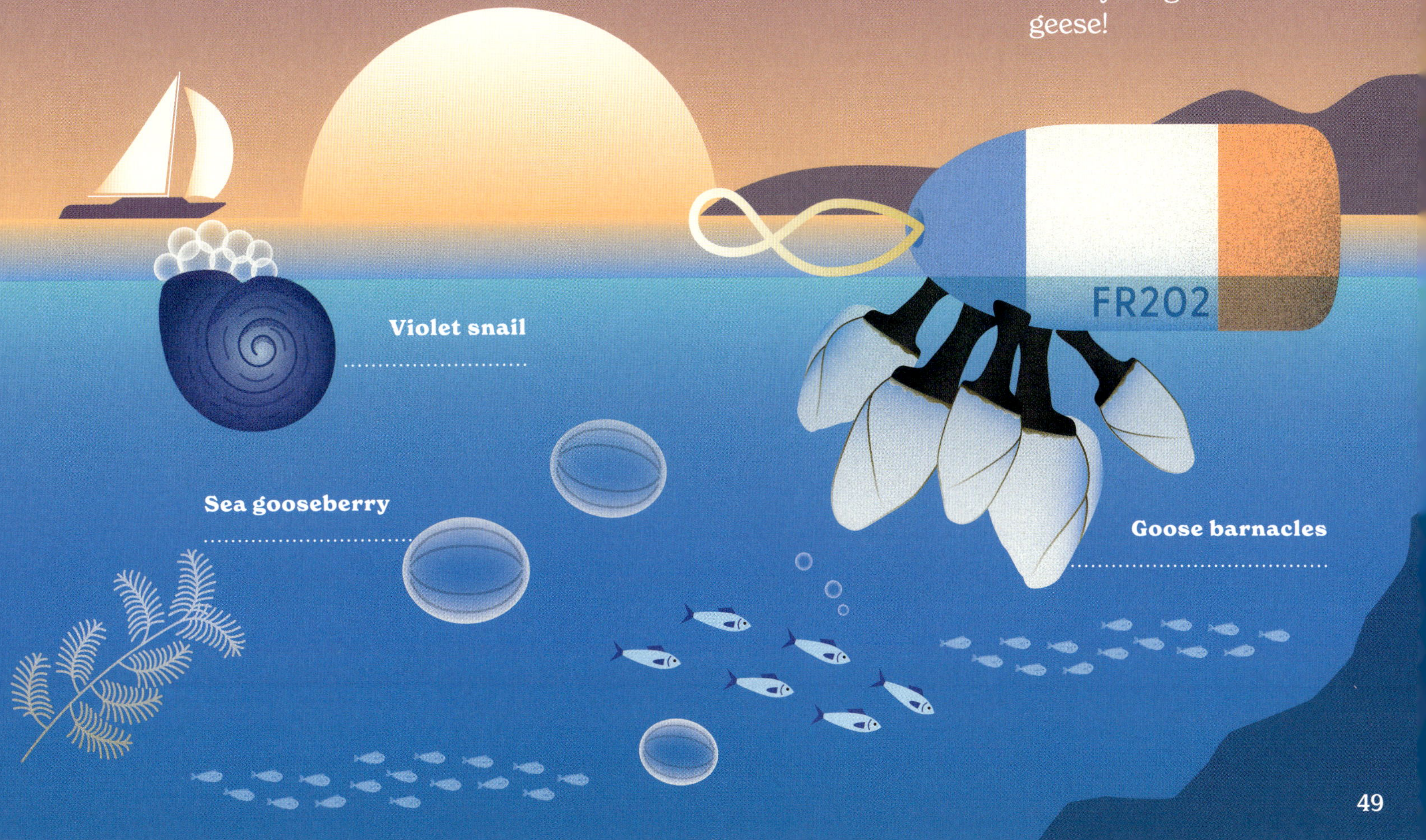

Plankton

Some of the most important plants and animals in the ocean are too small for us to see.

Drifters

Plankton comes from the Greek word for wander or drift and includes any plant or animal that cannot swim against tides and currents in the ocean (everything that swims – fish, whales, sharks, etc – is called nekton, which is from the Greek to swim).

Plankton are essential for a healthy ocean and for a healthy planet. Many plants and animals in the ocean spend a stage of their life floating as plankton. Others are plankton for their whole lives.

Seawater near the shore contains plankton that are too small for our eyes to see clearly. The amount in the water depends on the temperature of the water, the amount of food available, the season and whether or not the water has recently been mixed up by a storm. Some plankton can increase very quickly and become a bloom. When this happens, we might be able to see the plankton. For example, you might hear about red tides where thousands of microscopic plankton called dinoflagellates appear in an area. These dinoflagellates can be harmful for other marine life because they contain toxins. They can also cause harm because they use up all the oxygen in one part of the water.

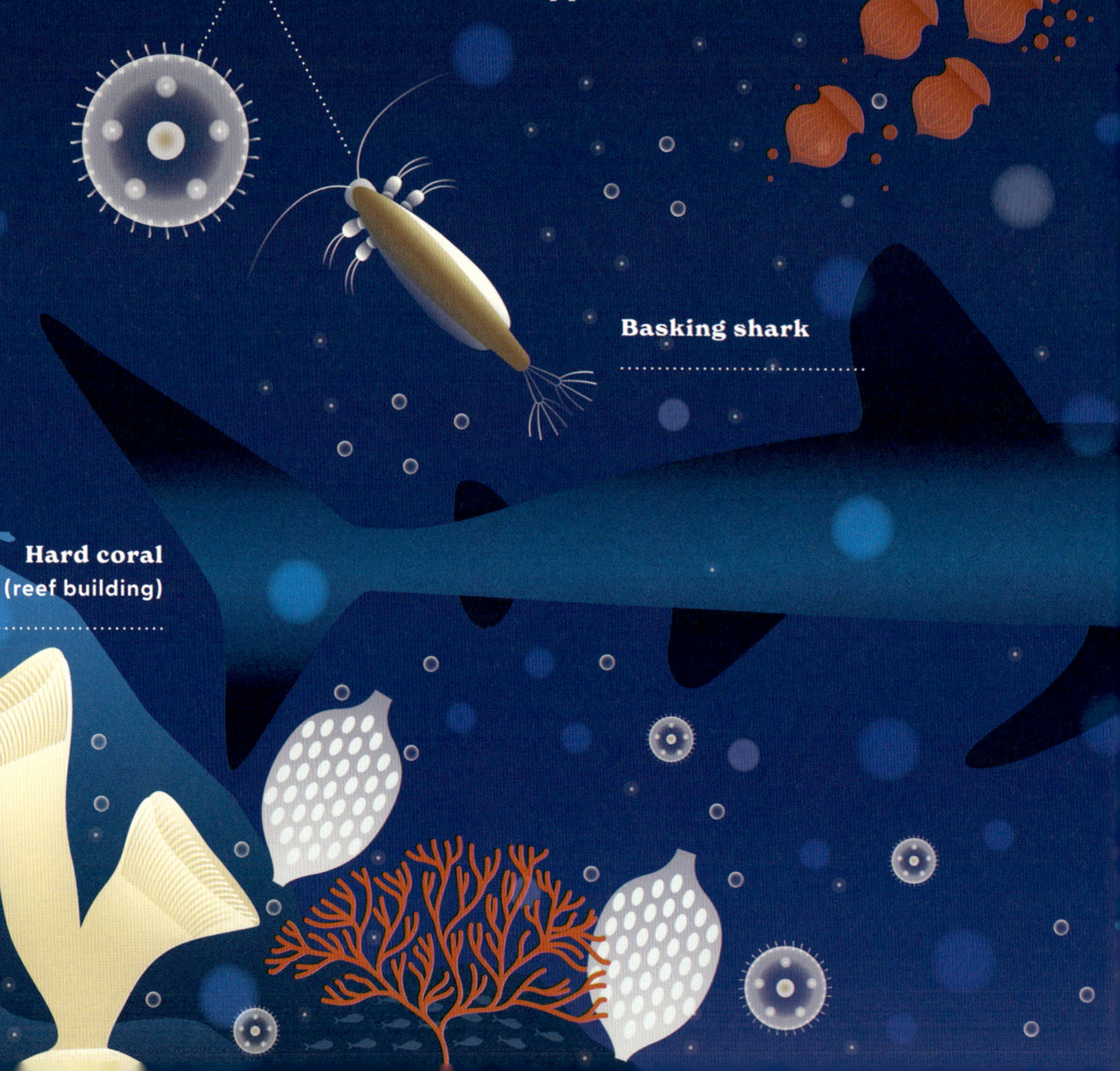

Sensitive life forms

In general, plankton will not cause you any harm. In fact, they are at the bottom of the marine food web and essential for life in the ocean. Plankton are also very sensitive to changes in climate, sea temperature, pollutants and many other things, so they can be used to show changes over time in the ocean, and also to monitor the health of life in an area of the ocean in general.

Bioluminescence

Bioluminescence

One of the most amazing things is that many species of plankton can create light. If you are lucky enough, you might be able to witness the seawater sparkling and flashing at night because the tiny plankton living in the water are sending out light signals to attract each other and warn off predators. Look for this sea sparkle in the autumn when it gets dark a bit earlier but the water is still warm. Plankton numbers will have increased over the summer and winter storms won't have mixed the water yet. Electrical lights and even a bright moon can prevent it being visible.

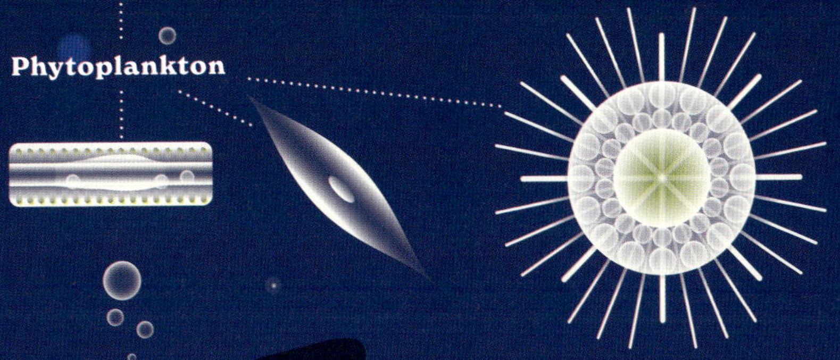

The seashore and us

As we live on an island, the sea has always been important for Irish people. In fact, it's how people first arrived here!

Our seashores
The coast as we know it today was probably formed over 10,000 years ago when the last ice age ended. This ice carved out many of our mountains and valleys. During the ice ages, millions of litres of water were held as frozen glaciers and ice sheets. When these melted, water flooded many of our valleys and separated islands from mainland Europe, and Ireland from Great Britain.

People have fished and foraged for food throughout Irish history. Things like seaweed, periwinkles and cockles are nutritious and fairly easy to find. Archaeologists have found piles of discarded seashells with signs that they were cooked and eaten thousands of years ago. Fishing continues to be an important activity in Ireland today.

The sea has also provided industry. For example, people used to harvest kelp and burn it in piles to create an ash they could sell to factories making soap, glass, dyes, bleaches and iodine for medicines. It is still used in the present day in foods for people and for animals. You've probably eaten or used something containing a chemical from seaweed today!

A seaweed illustration by Ellen Hutchins

Marine scientists

Ireland has also had many important marine scientists and explorers. Ellen Hutchins (1785–1815) was an important botanist (a person who studies plants). She specialised in non-flowering plants, including seaweeds. She was very talented at drawing seaweeds perfectly, before cameras were invented. She discovered many species that had not been recorded by scientists previously.

Maude Delap, a marine scientist who lived on Valentia Island in Kerry, was the first person to observe all the stages of the life cycle of a compass jellyfish. For many decades she also kept very important and detailed records of the plankton present in the water near her home. She discovered a very rare sea anemone that is still only found in one location, near Valentia Island.

Maude Delap

Lough Hyne is a very special saltwater lake in west Cork. It has been studied by scientists from all over the world and became the first marine nature reserve in Europe in 1981.

If you want to get involved in caring for the seashore, why not do a beach clean or join a Clean Coasts group? If you find something interesting on the seashore, you can report it to Biodiversity Ireland or even do one of their 'Explore your Shore' surveys.

Time to explore

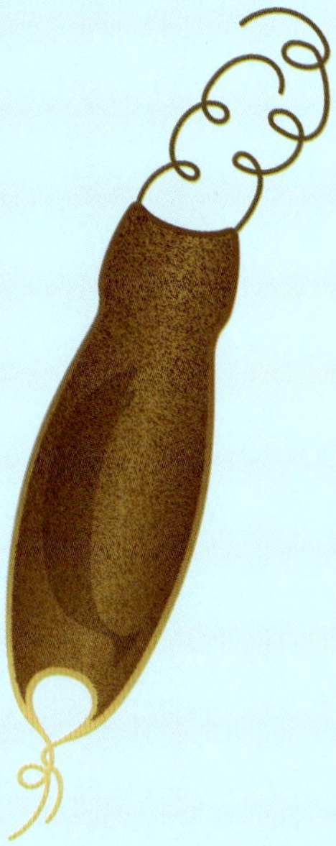

Next time you are at the seashore, keep an eye out for the species mentioned in this book! Put a tick next to each one you have seen.

Seashore plants

- [ ] Thrift
- [ ] Campion
- [ ] Sea samphire
- [ ] Sea beet
- [ ] Orache
- [ ] Sea mayweed
- [ ] Marram grass
- [ ] Sea sandwort
- [ ] Sea pinks
- [ ] Sea holly
- [ ] Sea bindweed

Flotsam, jetsam and natural treasures

- [ ] Sea beans
- [ ] Cuttlefish skeleton

Mermaid purses:

- [ ] Cat shark egg case
- [ ] Nursehound shark egg case
- [ ] Spotted skate egg case
- [ ] White skate egg case
- [ ] Blonde skate egg case
- [ ] Small eyed skate egg case
- [ ] Cuckoo skate egg case

Hoppers and crawlers

- [ ] Sand hopper
- [ ] Pill isopod
- [ ] Gammarid
- [ ] Sea slater

Cockles, clams and razor shells

- Cockle ☐
- Clam ☐
- Razor shell ☐
- Great scallop ☐
- Queen scallop ☐
- Prickly cockle ☐
- Surf clam ☐
- Banded wedge shell ☐
- Masked crab ☐
- Sea potato ☐
- Arctic cyprine ☐

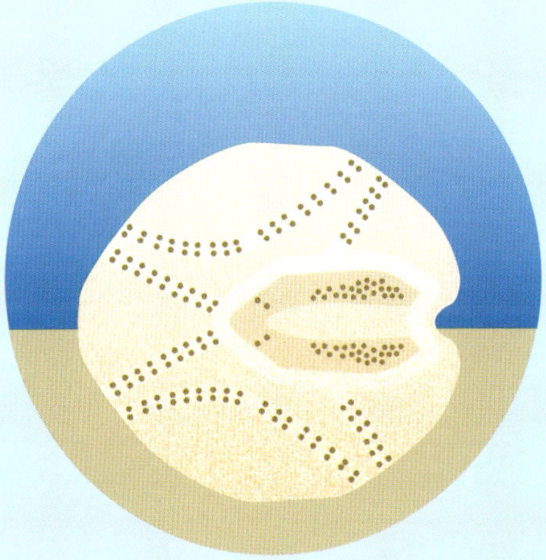

Crabs and shrimps

- Broad clawed porcelain crab ☐
- Lobster ☐
- Edible crab ☐
- Spiny spider crab ☐
- Shrimp ☐
- Prawn ☐
- Hermit crab ☐

Worms

- Lugworm ☐
- Ragworm ☐
- Bootlace worm ☐
- Sand mason ☐
- Tube worm ☐
- Green-leaf worm ☐
- Spiral worm ☐
- Honeycomb worm ☐
- Peacock worm ☐

Birds

- Black legged kittiwake ☐
- Iceland gull ☐
- Blackheaded gull ☐
- Curlew ☐
- Oystercatcher ☐
- Red-billed chough ☐
- Sandpiper ☐
- Ringed plover ☐
- Cormorant ☐
- Ringbilled gull ☐
- Great black-backed gull ☐
- Herring gull ☐
- Gannet ☐
- Puffin ☐
- Tern ☐
- Goose ☐

Seaweed

- Velvet horn ☐
- Horned wrack ☐
- Bladder wrack ☐
- Gutweed ☐
- Sea lettuce ☐
- Channelled wrack ☐
- Egg wrack ☐
- Oarweed ☐
- Strapweed ☐
- Carrageen ☐
- Sugar kelp ☐
- Dabberlocks ☐
- Spiral wrack ☐
- Sea beech ☐
- Furbelows ☐
- Thong weed ☐

Limpets, barnacles and mussels

- Acorn barnacle ☐
- Chiton ☐
- China limpet ☐
- Blue rayed limpet ☐
- Common limpet ☐
- Blue mussel ☐
- Horse mussel ☐

Sea snails

- Periwinkle ☐
- Purple topshell ☐
- Turban topshell ☐
- Painted topshell ☐
- Toothed topshell ☐
- Necklace shell ☐
- Dog whelk ☐
- Sea hare ☐
- Sea lemon ☐
- Cowry ☐

Butterflies

- Small blue ☐
- Grayling ☐

Mammals

- Harbour porpoise ☐
- Common dolphin ☐
- Bottlenose dolphin ☐
- Grey seal ☐
- Harbour seal ☐

Anemones

- Tiny beadlet anemone ☐
- *Sagartia elegans* ☐
- Beadlet anemone ☐
- Snakelocks anemone ☐
- Strawberry anemone ☐
- Dahlia anemone ☐

Sea squirts and sponges

- Breadcrumb sponge ☐
- Sea orange sponge ☐
- European sea squirt ☐
- Orange club sea squirt ☐
- Star ascidian sea squirt ☐
- Light blub sea squirt ☐
- Fluted sea squirt ☐
- Purse sponges ☐
- Encrusting sponges ☐
- Boring sponges ☐

Starfish and urchins

- Sea urchins ☐
- Common brittlestar ☐
- Green urchin ☐
- Common edible urchin ☐
- Common starfish ☐
- Purple urchin ☐
- Bloody henry ☐
- Cushion stars ☐

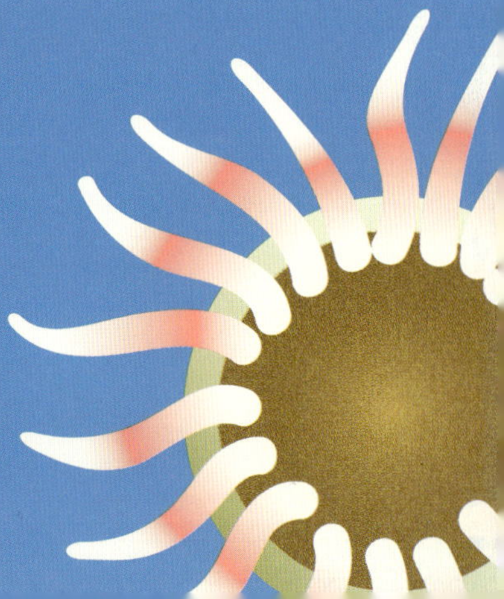

Fish

- Sand goby ☐
- Worm pipe fish ☐
- Butterfish ☐
- Shanny/Blennie ☐
- Five-bearded rockling ☐
- Two spotted goby ☐
- Lesser sand eel ☐
- Clingfish ☐
- Weever fish ☐
- Basking shark ☐

Jellyfish

- Blue jellyfish ☐
- Moon jellyfish ☐
- Mauve jellyfish ☐
- Barrel jellyfish ☐
- Compass jellyfish ☐
- Lion's mane jellyfish ☐

Drifters

- Sea gooseberry ☐
- Sunfish ☐
- Portuguese man o'war ☐
- By-the-wind-sailor ☐
- Violet snail ☐
- Goose barnacle ☐

Lucy Taylor lives beside the sea in County Kerry and is passionate about sharing her love for nature. She is a qualified marine biologist and has worked in education, research, SCUBA diving and nature conservation. She is the author of *Ireland's Seashore: A Field Guide*.

Linda Fährlin is an artist and illustrator inspired by the wild Atlantic Ocean and the landscape of the north-west of Ireland, where she lives. Previous books she has illustrated include *The Great Irish Science Book* and *The Illustrated Encyclopedia of Irish Lighthouses*.